AF411791

TROPICAL
RETREATS

THE POETICS OF PLACE

"Poetry is a soul inaugurating a form."
Pierre Jean Jouve

TROPICAL RETREATS

THE POETICS OF PLACE

TAN HOCK BENG

PAGE ONE PUBLISHING

TROPICAL RETREATS
THE POETICS OF PLACE

Published by:
Page One Publishing Pte Ltd
Block 4 Pasir Panjang Road
#06-35 Alexandra Distripark
Singapore 118491
Tel : 274 3188
Fax: 274 1833

Design :
K. C. Sin

Copy Editing:
Sheila Oliveiro

Production:
Maxim Ads Pte Ltd

Colour Separation:
Singapore Sang Choy Colour Separation Pte Ltd

Printer:
Toppan Printing Co (S) Pte Ltd

Printed in Singapore
ISBN: 981-00-8245-2

Frontispiece:
The Regent, Chiang Mai, Thailand

CONTENTS

INTRODUCTION

PAST AND PRESENCE IN
THE POETICS OF PLACE

" The taste of the apple . . . lies
in the contact of the fruit with the
palate, not in the fruit itself; in a similar
way. . . poetry lies in the meeting of the
poem and reader, not in the lines of
symbols printed on the pages of a book.
What is essential is the aesthetic act, the
thrill, the almost physical emotion that
comes with each reading."

Jorge Luis Borges,
Forward to Obra Poética

I t may seem axiomatic to define architecture as "one that evokes an emotional response and sensory experience." But architecture, as with all art, is inherently a sensual art. A major impact of architecture is the experiential, which can marshal a wide range of experiences. Every memorable encounter with architecture is multi-sensory, involving all realms of sensory experience which interact with each other simultaneously.

Traditional forms combine place-making and disciplined materiality in a sensual response to climate and context.

Previous page: Every memorable encounter with architecture is multi-sensory, involving all realms of sensory experience which interact with each other simultaneously. (Taman Mertasari, Sanur, Bali)

But we are now living in an era where much of the superficial pastiche found in current architectural production is regrettable. Traditional architecture demonstrates deep understanding of the psychological properties of materials, light and space. The grains of tropical hardwoods, the bubbly gurgle of delightful water features, or the soft diffused fall of light have all been eradicated in much of contemporary works.

In a world of flexible capital, continually blurring boundaries and globalization, contemporary architecture has abandoned construction and materiality in favour of a scenographic approach. As Christian Norberg-Schulz argues, "A phenomenology of place . . . has to comprise the basic modes of construction and their relationship to formal articulation. Meaning and character cannot be interpreted in purely formal or aesthetic terms, but are . . . intimately connected with making."[1]

The consumerist gloss, while flattening everything out, produces an architecture that is rapidly detaching itself from the invisible sensory realms to a purely visual one. But as Ungers defines it : "Architecture acts as an intellectual bridge between the *visible* and the *invisible*, the *corporeal* and the *formless*, the *expressible* and the *effable;* it affirms the analogical correspondence of the order of reality; it is intended to function both physically and metaphysically . . . The architectural work embodies in a tangible form . . . what is intangible and incorporeal."

In an age increasingly dominated by the transient vacuities of cyberspace, the visible has assumed greater importance over the invisible and the unquantifiable. The architect's role has been largely marginalised to being cosmeticians of the buildings' skins. The image-laden pastiches of Postmodernism continue to proliferate, reflecting an economy of instant gratification. Historicism gains new grounds, while the fragmented aesthetic of Deconstructivism, transplanted from the fields of French philosophy and literary criticism in the late 1960s, continues to express the perceived confusion and instability in our society.

Many of these works are essentially scenographic, and thereby easily reproduced. This quick turnover of images, aptly termed "the consumeristic amortization of the built environment" by Kenneth Frampton, as well as the easy spread of imagery promulgated by the Eurocentric architectural media, promote architecture as fashion for popular consumption. The 'look' predominates over all other forms of sensual engagement.

Frederic Jameson argues that we have ventured into an age where cultural production "has become integrated into commodity production generally; the frantic urgency of producing fresh waves of ever more novel seeming goods, at ever greater rates of turnover, now assigns an increasingly essential structural function to aesthetic innovation and experimentation." He sees "depthlessness" as "perhaps the supreme formal feature" of this new mentality that celebrates difference and spectacle. [2]

Architecture is about creating crafted physical, as well as mental space, like this traquil pool at Amandari, Bali. Its strong visceral quality has spawned a number of progeny and its variations.

It is not difficult to recognise those elusive qualities in tropical architecture – in particular those which are independent of stylistic expressions – in fact, to feel their very palpability.

Architectural aesthetics has become an *anaesthetic play* that in effect dulls the senses. Buildings have walls serving as a paper-thin veneer, with borrowed or arbitrary motifs totally unrelated to the means of construction, or to any meaningful experience of the building. Architecture is literally marginalised to the design of the first few millimetres of skins while architects have reduced themselves to manipulators of gratuitous imagery. No one has written more cogently of this rift than Juhani Pallasmaa, who points out : "Our relation to physical reality keeps weakening and we live increasingly in a world of dreams, in a stream of unrelated sensory impressions."[3]

The book is essentially a personal snapshot of moods and poetic dimensions found in some of the more sensual works in the region. Demonstrating an absence of fussy frippery, these works are important signposts for an architecture of the senses. They are delightful syntheses of simple materiality, consummate craftsmanship and rich moods. Some are humble structures while others are palatial complexes. Together, they truly evoke an architecture of empathy and resonance, one that grounds their inhabitants in the specificity of place.

In Asia, the cultures are vigorous. This wondrous region is rich with traditional architecture that marvellously makes places. Traditional forms combine place-making and disciplined materiality in a sensual response to such basic determinants as climate, context and technology. The built works are invariably tectonic, with an inescapable sense of the tactile.

New generation architects are reinterpreting the sensuality of traditional precedents to create contemporary works that heighten the non-reducible experiences of life.

One of the contemporary paradoxes is that the pressures of globalisation and universal commodification confront ever more intense awareness of the local. However it is extremely difficult to find appropriate contemporary models that are brilliant syntheses of regional traditions and innovative abstraction. The projects featured here are isolated examples in a sea of

The ineffable phenomena of light, shadows and moods contribute greatly to a sensual experience of tropicality.

either excessive sentimentality or banal Post-Modernist kitsch. Admitedly, there is a lack of "critical appropriation". Superficial allusionism is still all too common. But beyond the images, many of these projects achieve intensity and integrity. They evoke deep resonances, revealing the tectonic and tactile dimensions.

House in Batujimbar, Bali.

The allusive poetics and corporeal presence of these spaces offer great pleasure. One recalls at this juncture Gaston Bachelard 's highly influential and insightful book – *The Poetics of Space* – where he reminds us that the "soul inaugurates. Here it is the supreme power. It is human dignity. Even if the "form" was already well-known, previously discovered, carved from 'commonplaces,' before the interior poetic light was turned upon it, it was a mere object for the mind. But the soul comes and inaugurates the form, dwells in it, takes pleasure in it."[4]

Architecture is not merely an operational necessity by which to satisfy pragmatic requirements. It is about creating crafted physical, as well as mental space. In the latter, literal images and abstract images dwell together with moods and emotions. Tadao Ando has described his own works as "an architecture created with all experiences from all facets of life, a universe where the wind brings happiness, and where one feels happy to be alive."

The book hopes to present - inadequate of course, but more like a glimpse – elusive qualities in tropical architecture, in particular those which are relatively independent of stylistic expressions – the ineffable phenomena of materials and moods. Sharing the late Mexican architect Luis Barragan's concern for "an emotional piece of architecture, not a cold piece of convenience", the book comprises impressionistic samples of recurrent themes that are unmistakably manifest in a multi-dimensional way.

The book has been greatly inspired by a remarkably perceptive essay by Pallasmaa. His "Six Themes For The Next Millennium", based on the Herman Miller Lecture given at the Royal Institute of British Architects in London in 1994, which was subsequently published in *The Architectural Review* in July 1994, was an important starting point for this book.

The allusive poetics and corporeal presence of sensual spaces llike those found in this house at Batujimbar, Bali, offer great pleasure.

In the essay, Pallasmaa laments the narcissism and self-indulgence of much of contemporary works. He argues that "reversion to images of a lost past in architecture is grounded in the very strategy of capitalist economy; the whole of history becomes a market place; local and ethnic traditions and historical settings are fabricated under the disguise of a search for roots. Thematisation is the newest strategy of persuasion, of directing and controlling emotional response, by detaching imagery from its spontaneous autonomy; the image is not allowed to arise from within but it is forced into a preconceived interpretation." [5]

Pallasmaa further proposes that in an increasingly frenetic world, existential meanings of inhabiting space can be wrought by the art of architecture alone. He suggests six themes for the "re-enchantment" of architecutre at the turn of the millennium. These are: Slowness, Plasticity, Sensuousness, Authenticity, Idealisation, Silence.

These themes provide a broad framework in which the book is organised. The sensual aspects of architecture in the tropics, which are multivalent and engage our full bodily participation, are hence grouped into several themes that provide a shared ground. Ranging from tactility to tranquillity, they are of course, very abstractly stated. But it is certainly not hard to recognise, in fact, to even feel their very palpability.

Remarkably, such themes, though common, are rarely discussed. This is probably because they are extremely difficult to record or be communicated. Kisho Kurokawa shares the same sentiment when he claims that "in every culture there are states or atmospheres or concepts which cannot be logically explained, and their very ineffability makes them vulnerable to extinction . . . Unlike concepts, sensations are much harder to identify and explain. But this is only fitting, for by trying to analyse and discuss sensations, we only constrain their spontaneity and betray their inherent naturalness. But even as I say this, I want to talk about sensation, because rather than simply succumbing to the embrace of a sensation, I believe there is self-discovery in grappling with the discordant impulses it creates in the mind." [6]

The sensual aspects of architecture in the tropics are multivalent and engage our full bodily participation.

At the same time, the book's herculean task is to capture, through its two-dimensionality, the world of senses which constitute the very essence of tropical architecture. It can never be completely explicable. Ezra Stoller, the undisputed modern master of architectural photography observes that photography is a limited medium : "An architectural photograph can never do more than suggest a part of that space in a segment of time . . . As interpreters with cameras we are called upon to resolve a myriad of conflicting conditions in terms of an extremely limited medium and to communicate a four-dimensional experience (yes, time is one of the elements involved) with a flat piece of paper and restricted tonal palette."

An architecture of empathy and resonance embraces a whole spectrum of design elements, ranging from the tectonic dimension to the use of nature.

Most of the photographs shown here are taken out of their specific contexts. The purpose is to interpret, emphasise, accentuate and elucidate particular qualities of different buildings. Constant in these photographs is also a heightened sense of pleasure. In all the buildings featured, the pleasure and passion - of the designer, the builder and the occupant - are tangibly evident. As Herman Hesse declares : "The beginning of all art is love, the value and scope of all art are determined by the artist's capacity for love." The patron saint of art, which includes architecture, is Passion. Art critic Alvar Gonzalez-Palacios has also written of his art, "... we recall that the secret of poetry lies not so much in the poetic object as in the heart of the poet who loves." Jeff Wall, who is probably the most important contemporary artist using photography as a medium, makes the claim that "a successful picture is a source of pleasure and I believe that it is the pleasure experienced in art that makes possible any critical reflection about its subject matter or forms." It is also hoped that a new generation of architects will reinterpret the sensuality to create architecture for contemporary needs that touch our most fundamental feelings and heighten the non-reducible experiences of life. We need an architecture that opens up ever new ways to the senses.

Traditional architecture demonstrates deep understanding of the psychological properties of materials, light and space.

Some of the sensual works in the region are delightful syntheses of simple materiality and consummate craftsmanship, like this art piece designed by Bensley Design Group for a resort in Bali.

Footnotes:

1 Christian Norberg-Schulz, *Genius Loci: Towards a Phenomenology of Architecture*, New York: Rizzoli International Publications, Inc., 1980, pp. 65-66.

2 Frederic Jameson, "Postmodernism, Or The Cultural Logic of Late Capitalism", *New Left Review* 146 (July-August 1984), pp. 53-92.

3 Juhani Pallasmaa, "Six Themes For The Next Millennium" in *The Architectural Review*, July 1994 pp. 77

4 Gaston Bachelard, *The Poetics of Space*, Beacon Press, Boston.

5 Juhani Pallasmaa, "Six Themes For The Next Millennium", pp. 75.

6 Kishio Kurokawa, "Rikyu Gray and the Art of Ambiguity" in *The Japan Architect*, June 1979, pp. 23

The wondrous regions of Asia are rich with traditional architecture that marvellously makes places, like this water spout in Bali.

In an increasingly frenetic world, existential meanings of inhabiting space can be wrought by the art of architecture alone. (Amankila, Bali, Indonesia)

TACTILITY

"Beyond architecture, our culture at large seems to drift towards a distancing, a kind of chilling, de-sensualization and de-eroticization of the human relation to reality."

Juhani Pallasmaa

The concept of tactility is an important part of our intimate engagement with architecture.

Opposite: Tactility brings us back to the world of touch and emotions, like this wall in Villa Bebek, Sanur, Bali.

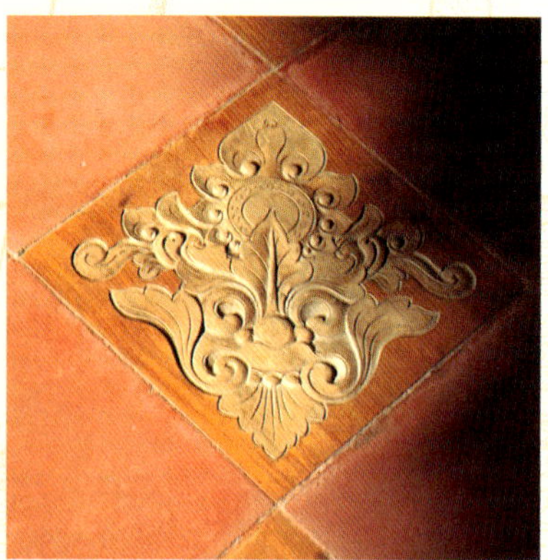

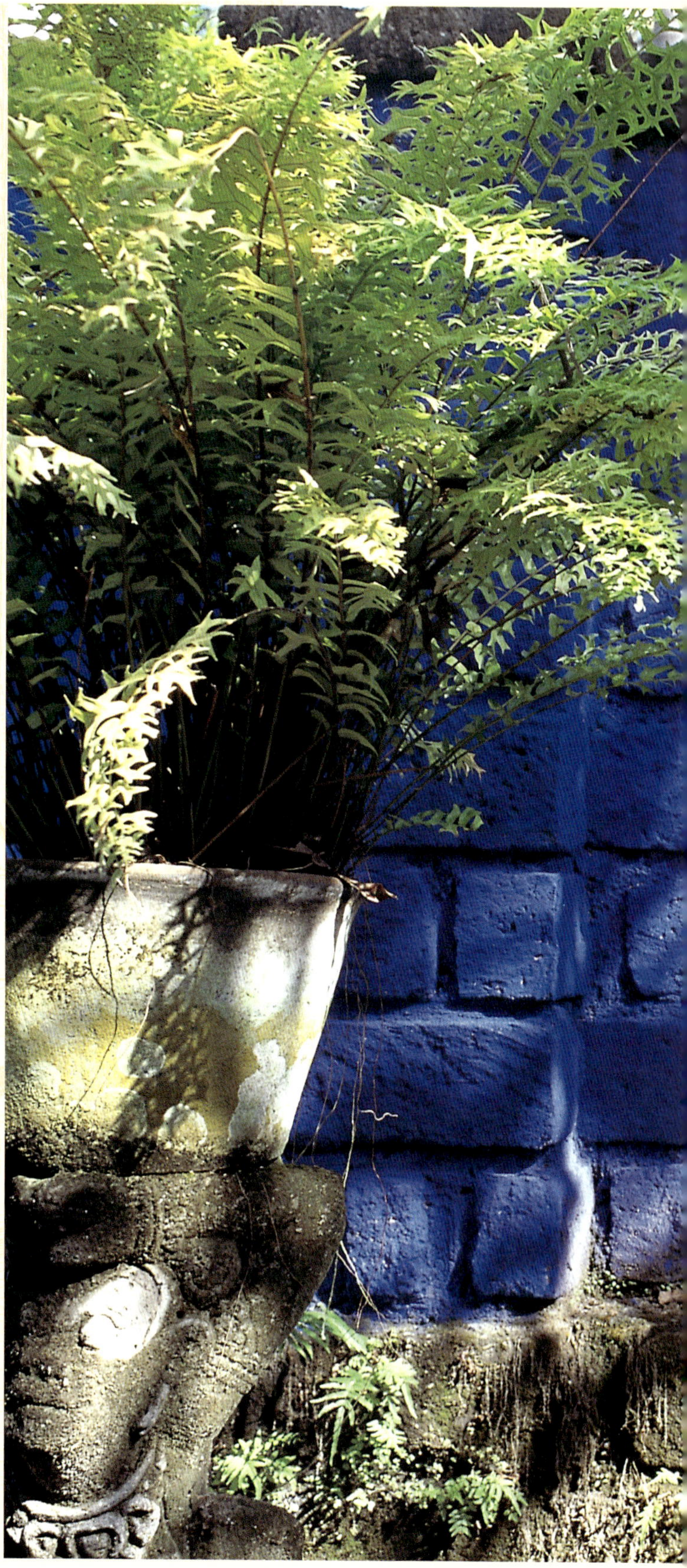

Sensibility or "sensorial perception" is the direct stimulation of the senses, as opposed to rational perception. The tactile brings us back to the world of touch, smell and emotions. It invokes a range of sensuous experience - like smooth versus rough and distended versus recessed. Such binary stimuli bring us fully into the world of sensory perceptions.

The concept of non-retinal sensations, like the smell of timber and the touch of stonework, is an important part of our intimate engagement with architecture. This tactile understanding of reality has been remarked on by Tadao Ando : "The body articulates the world. At the same time, the body is articulated by the world. When "I" perceive the concrete to be something cold and hard, "I" recognise the body as something warm and soft. In this way the body in its dynamic relationship with the world becomes the *shintai*. It is only the *shintai* in this sense that builds or understands architecture. The *shintai* is a sentient being that responds to the world." [1]

Such a phenomenological awareness has been much eroded in contemporary architecture. This loss of tactility and the tectonic dimension has been lamented by many critics. But no one has argued more persuasively than Pallasmaa, one of the chief proponents for a tactile architecture and its material expression. He points out that "with the loss of tactility and the scale and details crafted for the human body and hand, our structures become repulsively flat, sharp-edged, immaterial, and unreal. The detachment of construction from the realities of matter and craft turns architecture into stage sets for the eye, devoid of authenticity of material and tectonic logic." [2]

Buildings have in general become two-dimensional projections of plans, with the craft of construction – the nineteenth-century Germanic notion of *Formgefühl* – rapidly losing ground.

A re-immersion in the sensual world is necessary.

Tactile, delectable surfaces can be appreciated by anyone. Materials, in their raw state, stimulate the senses. They express their material essence as well as their age. The texture of exposed stone, for example, is infinitely pleasurable. Textures also affect our gait, and hence the way we move through a space and how we experience it.

In the traditional architecture of the region, tactility is used to evoke a phenomenological awareness.

Materials are also testaments to the effects of the elements and the passage of time, and hence evoking a phenomenological awareness. Steven Holl penetratingly observes that "the architectural transformations of natural materials, such as glass or wood, have dynamic thought and-sense-provoking qualities. The materials communicate in resonance and dissonance, as do musical instruments. Like instruments of woodwind, brass, and percussion, their orchestration in an architectural composition is crucial to the perception and communication of ideas, as the orchestration of instruments is to a symphonic work."[3]

One of the intrinsic qualities of architecture is its expressiveness of its own nature as constructional elements put together in defiance of gravity. This sense of tectonic quality and tactility, part of what Vitruvius meant by *firmitas*, has been highly developed in the vernacular architecture of Asia. Ordinary materials are used

for their expressive capacity. The once abundant teak forests in northern Thailand, for example, have allowed extensive use of wood in traditional architecture and decoration. A number of other hardwoods like cengal and ironwood were also much used. Timber was hence given an intensely tactile quality, and which with time was developed into a construction process of great subtlety.

Appreciation of such tactility was poetically expressed by Anais Nin when she described Tandjung Sari, the forerunner of exquisite retreats in Bali : "The separate bungalows were built in native style and set in opulent gardens . statues of gods and goddesses appeared in niches. The room, with its split bamboo walls, mats, rafts, poles tied together with bark fibre, gave off vibrations which I can only describe as similar to those one feels in a forest, as if natural materials never lost their power to conduct life . . ."

Timber and bamboo are among the most common building materials.

The need for tactility is one of the primal psychological urges that have been basic to man since time immemorial. Inspired by the time-honoured simplicity of traditional Asian architecture and combined with a proclivity for the tactile, many architects practising in the region today are discernibly making a return to the poetic formal and tactile dimensions. In the more sensitively designed of contemporary works, thoughtful and sensual exploration of materials is evident. The character and integrity of materials are expressively brought out in an undisguised, and sometimes even effusive, attempt at recovering the loss in sensory intimacy and gratification.

Footnotes:

1   Tadao Ando, "Shintai and Space" in *Architecture and Body*, New York : Rizzoli, 1988.

2   Juhani Pallasmaa, "An Architecture of the Seven Senses" in *Questions of Perception*, A+U Architecture and Urbanism, July 1994 Special Issue, pp. 29

Materials are testaments to the effects of the elements and the passage of time.

Left & right: In Asia, the use of timber has been developed into a construction process of great subtlety.

This relief at The Regent Chiang Mai is a wonderful example of simple materiality and superb craftsmanship.

Designed by Bensley Design Studio, this water feature at Karawawaci Golf & Country Club in Jakarta, Indonesia, is a delightful synthesis of the tectonic and the tactile.

Set in Ubud, the artistic heart of Bali, this resort is a tantalisingly escapist sanctuary. Its greatest asset is probably the fact that it enjoys an extraordinarily stunning site that overlooks the Petanu River, which is one of the holiest rivers in Bali. Many sacred sanctuaries had been built along its steep banks.

Surrounded by verdant rice terraces, the presence of the green essence of the landscape is pervasive. Touted as a "Sanctuary for the Senses", the resort's name represents everlasting hope and beauty. Appropriately, the resort has a grandeur expressly designed for the majesty of the setting and the poignancy of its name.

Kamandalu consists of 58 individual villas built in traditional Balinese style with outdoor showers, open-sided pavilions, private courtyards and landscaped gardens. In this respect, the typology adopted is one that that has already been well established by significant Balinese precedents like the Amandari and the Four Seasons Jimbaran. Enclosed behind high walls, some of these villas have their own intimate swimming pools and jacuzzis overlooking spectacular rice terraces and emerald forests that shimmer with a particular radiance in the late light of the day.

In the villa, wide sliding glass panels bring the outdoors into the interior. The tone of enchanted elegance continues in the use of muted colours and understated upholstery. Used to offset the richness of timber, the finishes and their exquisite materiality give the interiors an intimate feel.

The Banyan Tree Kamandalu is a densely rich landscape of retreat and renewal, offering both visual calmness and sensory pleasure. It is a picturesque ideal that has been superbly crafted by the consummate skills of Balinese builders. The palpability of unadulterated materials is a joy to experience.

Each individual villa is enclosed by high walls.

Opposite: The tactile quality of the finishes is tangibly evident.

In the Pool Villa, a huge pool overlooks the verdant valleys.

A garden pavilion is surrounded by a free-form pool.

Existing structures have been renovated to blend with the new layout.

View of the Pool Villa from the swimming pool.

Previous page: View from the Restaurant Pavilion.

The reception lobby is one of the many older structures that have been recently renovated.

The bathroom enjoys a view of the private courtyard.

Top: Interior view of a typical Villa.

Lanna, or "Land of a Million Rice Fields", is the name by which the northern part of Thailand and its unique culture have been known for centuries. Founded in 1296 by King Mengrai, the Lanna Kingdom was greatly influenced by neighbouring Burma, China, Laos and Yunnan. Its distinctive traditions are still apparent in the modern city of Chiang Mai. Located about 700 km north of Bangkok, this second largest city of Thailand is largely noted for both its cultural heritage and cool climate.

Fondly referred to by the Thais as the "Rose of the North", this beautiful city is situated about 310 metres above sea level and has long been a favourite holiday resort for Thais and foreigners alike. Over the last couple of years, many holiday homes and resorts have been built in the green valleys outside the city.

The Regent, which opened in April 1995, clearly stands out as one of the most outstanding projects in this fertile intermontane basin. The Masterplan was conceptualised by Thai architect Lek Bunnag

and Bangkok-based landscape architect Bill Bensley. It clearly demonstrates an earnest concern and a keen sensitivity to the pristine environment. Located in the sub-municipality of Mae Rim District, the city's first five-star resort is only 13 km from Chiang Mai.

Architect Chulathat Kitibutr of Chiangmai Architects Collaborative borrowed elements from the rich cultural heritage of northern Thailand in the design of the luxurious resort. Formulated on a solid underpinning of architectural knowledge, the resort essentially comprises 16 double-storey clusters of four rooms with attached outdoor pavilions.

The prominent, intricately carved crossed bargeboards or *kaelae* and private gazebos called *salas* formed part of the design of the

The Spa Pavilion is located next to the pool.

Opposite: Accommodation are housed in double-storey clusters of 4 rooms with attached outdoor pavilions or salas.

Next page: A view of the reception lobby at night.

Landscape features incorporate the use of water throughout the undulating terrain.

well-crafted guest pavilions. Overlooking the dramatic Doi Suthep mountains, these raised teak pavilions are integrated with eight hectares of rice terraces and lush landscaped gardens. The bold use of the rice fields as part of the landscaping strategy is not only unique, but it also brings the resort back to the region's agricultural roots. The rice harvested is distributed to charity and hill-tribe villages.

Several consultants collaborated in the execution of this exquisite *tour de force*. The carefully crafted interiors are designed by John Lightbody of Abacus Design, while the landscape design is by Bill Bensley of Bensley Design Group Studios. The landscape is probably the most important and memorable element in the resort. Tropical vegetation is celebrated in a manner that can perhaps be best described as one of unbridled enthusiasm and controlled planting, and a sense of the natural with a deliberate sense of artificiality. Linked by paths made of sandstone laterite, the various amenities of the

resort are hidden by thick foliage. This lush tropical environment is full of little surprises. The varied and manifold delights of the gardens are a pleasure to experience. Careful placement of sculptural artefacts and terracotta reproductions of Khmer art works in the nooks and corners of the grounds enhance the overall effect. At every turn, these unexpected objects surprise and amuse.

The late Egyptian architect Hassan Fathy once argued that "when the full power of the human imagination is backed by the weight of a living tradition, the resulting work of art is much greater than any that an artist can achieve when he has no tradition in which to work or when he wilfully abandons his traditions." In this age of massive technological achievements, the Regent Chiang Mai demonstrates that vernacular traditions are still thankfully seen as having an important influence on the conscience of many Asian architects who are resisting Western hegemony and the homogenisation of world cultures.

View of the water court from the lobby.

Top: Sculptural artefacts are placed all over the grounds.

The various amenities of the resort are hidden by thick foliage.

Carvings of elephants mark the entrance to the car court.

Wooden figurines flanked a stairway.

Opposite: A gazebo is located next to the restaurant.

Set amid the same idyll environment as The Regent, these luxurious properties have an arresting presence. Expressive of an individual sensibility, this is a condominium development that offers privacy combined with the benefits and convenience of the resort's restaurants, room service and selected facilities. There is also a private swimming pool for the exclusive use of owners and guests.

The estate is located on a 20-acre (60 *rai*) of lush greenery, with the nearby misty hills forming a picturesque backdrop. Surrounded by teak trees, it comprises 24 luxury units in 10 separate villas. These 3 or 4-storey villas are concerted exercises in form-making. They are highly articulated and carefully proportioned, in an obvious attempt at breaking down the scale. Designed by Lek Bunnag of Bunnag Architects, who is a forceful talent to be watched, the units range in size from approximatey 330 square metres to 445 square metres. These are offered in three different layouts – Garden Terrace, Mountain View and Penthouse. The Garden units have their own individual plunge pools, while the penthouses occupy the top two floors of each villa. Spiral staircases lead up to open-sided pavilions at the top.

Architectural proportion and vocabulary are intensively explored in a celebratory manner. Elements are cleverly juggled together, espe-

Top & bottom: An interesting series of roofscapes can be found at The Residences.

View of the 4-storey Residences from the swimming pool.

cially the way steeply pitched roofs are juxtaposed. Ornate latticework and rubbled walls give it a quaintly Oriental imagery that is unique. The masonry base gives it the reassuring *gravitas* of heaviness and age while the spires and roof finials provide the necessary lightness and elegance.

The eclecticism and studied complexity extend to the interiors as well, where wood is used extensively. Richly patterned and extraordinarily wrought details are employed to convey this sense of Orientalism. Immaculate craftsmanship, apparent throughout the development, is a constant pleasure. All of the setting's lush beauty can be enjoyed through large openings everywhere. Every unit is fitted with a large, open kitchen and custom-designed terrazo baths. A fireplace gives the living room a reassuring solidity and warmth.

The Residences is a provocative piece of work in more ways than one. An assured piece of architecture, it has an innate vigour that is perhaps derived from the intense effort put into the design. The effect is made much more dramatic at night when the silhouette of the multi-tiered roofs invoke an aura of histrionics.

The end result of the bricolaged aesthetic provokes ambivalence. At one level, the project might be perceived as a hedonistic and outlandish piece of strange collage, inclining precipitously close to the decorative. Yet one witnesses the masterful execution of various 'styles' into a convincing whole. Rather than being a quotational ploy, the project is a result of a liberal dose of Bunnag's personal sensibility. The spirit of intuitive invention is wonderfully evident. A fond ode to the enigmatic landscape, this project has a refreshing and compelling vitality wholly its own.

Elements are cleverly juggled together.

Pavilions are hidden behind lush foliage.

Opposite: Proportion and architectural vocabulary are intensively explored in an obvious attempt at breaking down the scale of the complex.

Surrounded by teak trees, the Residences comprises 24 luxury units.

The project is a fond ode to the enigmatic land-scape.

The masonry base gives the building a sense of heaviness.

Every unit has a small entrance lobby that overlooks the lush greenery.

The eclecticism extends to the interiors as well, where the fireplace is the central focus.

Top: View of the Residences from the Regent.

LIGHTNESS

"Someone guides us through its spaces. We glide along. Talking seems superfluous; everything is unique, yet never demanding."

Alvaro Siza

Elegant loftiness and lightness of a traditional Thai roof.

Opposite: The lightness of the thatched roof is further reinforced by the use of water features.

Kenneth Frampton, in his incisive book *Studies in Tectonic Culture*, argues that the "opposition between the culture of the light and the culture of the heavy will manifest itself to different degrees in different cultures, with certain societies tending to be either exclusively stereotomic or exclusively tectonic in character, as in, say, the pyramids of Mesoamerica in the first instance or the timber building cultures of Southeast Asia in the second. In many cultures, including that of China, one will find a typical opposition between a heavyweight masonry podium and a lightweight timber roof floating over it..."[1]

Traditional Southeast Asian architecture is particularly characterised by the use of stilts. With the exception of Bali, parts of Java and the coastal region of Vietnam, the whole of Southeast Asia has houses raised high on stilts.

These dwellings evoke a sense of weightlessness and flotation. They also make full use of the tectonic expressivity of timber. Most of these structures are variants of a post-and-beam system of construction. They utilise a timber syntax comprising of lightweight, linear interlocking components which can be used to create a wide variety of forms. Such a "tectonics of the frame" usually consists of either a sagging beamwork technique, in which the wood is compressed vertically, or the radiating beamwork technique, where wood is compressed obliquely.

The wall is generally not an important building element in Southeast Asia. Hence the use of load-bearing walls, with their resultant stereotomic quality, is uncommon. The frame system is the main building component that contributes to a general sense of lightness. The

The use of thatched roofing materials is a traditional Balinese architectural feature.

The 'floating' roof form appears to hover above the solid masonry base.

The structure is almost entirely made up of thatch, yet it exudes a sense of immateriality.

soaring temples of Thailand, with their sweeping, graceful curves, have an airy sense of lightness, while the raised houses of traditional dwellings in many parts of Asia have an elegant loftiness. Vertiginous effects are emphasised by the slenderness of timber supports. The effects of light filtering in from the top also contribute greatly to the sense of loftiness.

Interestingly, this quality is sometimes greatly enhanced by the introduction of heavy masonry podiums. In Balinese architecture, for example, hovering roofs supported by slender timber posts resting on solid masonry bases set up an opposition that evokes a particular sense of equipoise. Articulation of joints, usually notched or scooped, is of primary importance to the expressivity of form. The visual result can be very striking.

Such 'weightless' effects also evoke cosmic and other animistic associations. In many Southeast Asian societies, the house is seen as an animate entity. Extended ridge-lines and outward-sloping gable-ends can be commonly found in various dwelling types in Indonesia. A symbol of the Thai house which gives it a characteristic sense of lightness is the barge-board which closes off the end of the roof rafters extending beyond the gable. This is called *pan-lom* in Thai, which means "shaping the wind". Another recurring feature is the decorative gable-finials, which can be found in North Thailand and Indonesia. The meeting of the roof

Opposite: Sailing gable-end details of the roof structures at the Club Med in Maldives.

and the sky is thus given added phenomenological significance through such elaborately carved elements.

An elaborate bracketing system supports this multi-tiered roof structure.

Bottom: The use of dried leaves provide an interesting counterpoint to the timber shingles.

The design and finishes of the roof also impart an overall sense of lightness. It is usually covered with plant materials like grass, woven palm frond matting, or bamboo. Grass, especially the popular *Imperata cylindrica* species (*alang-alang* in Indonesian), are commonly used for thatching. The elegance and simplicity of these materials have a corporeal impact.

To sum up, a visual relationship between the architectural object and the perceiving subject is set up through three sensibilities : an emphasis on lighweight construction, the use of materials and the effects of light on it. Such poetic fusions of light and materiality provide invaluable lessons for contemporary architects seeking to infuse their works with a sense of lightness. As Pallasmaa proposes, "Architecture must again learn to speak of materiality, gravity and the tectonic logic of its own making."[2]

Footnotes:

1   Kenneth Frampton, *Studies in Tectonic Culture*, MIT Press, 1995, pp. 248

2   Juhani Pallasmaa, "Six Themes For The Next Millennium" pp. 75,

All: In Thai architecture, the meeting of roof and sky is given added phenomenological significance through elaborately carved barge-boards.

A pervasive sense of lightness is evident at the Ibah in Bali

Located just off the west coast of the Malay Peninsula, the Pangkor Laut Resort is set on a 121-ha hilly island, amid an enchanting environment of lush rainforests and vast expanses of white sandy beaches. Designed by the Bangkok-based architecture firm of Bunnag Architects and landscape practice of Bensley Design Group, this project is a superb demonstration of the pair's propensity for seeking strong spatial solutions.

The tranquil resort is a delightful result of architect Lek Bunnag's scrupulousness and confident articulation of space and materials. Highly animated by an interplay of solidity and transparency, the resort's accommodation is in Royal and Coral Bays. The former has 53 private villas. Of these, 23 are set on stilts over the sea. They are linked to one another and to the island by a timber walkway. There are 59 units at Coral Bay. Some of the private villas are set on stilts over the water while others are built on the hillsides.

The villas, especially, exhibit a marked tectontic sensibility. Each is a product of deft hands and sure eyes. Designed with an organisational simplicity in mind, the artificial separation of inside from outside is broken down. Having meticulously resolved the pragmatic concerns, Bunnag's inclination for the expressive probity of natural materials is also evident.

Inspired by Thai and Indonesian precedents, details are reinterpreted in a new light. Bamboo and plywood are used for the ceilings while belian wood is used as roofing materials.

The honed simplicity of details and the understanding of materiality result in a tactile architecture that thrills the senses and allow for a full set of experiences. Permeated with light, the entire resort reverberates with a certain luminosity. It is an eloquent reminder of the delight of lightness in architecture.

This is a lucid and precise work, one where the experiential aspects are of greater significance than its imagery of the romantic ideal and tropical vitality. It is sensorially strong because kinetic activities are harnessed in a perceptibly complex circulation route.

The client's intention is to enhance Malay cultural heritage through a reinterpretation of traditional architecture.

Villas are set on stilts over the sea and connected to one another and to the island by wooden walkways.

The honed simplicity of
details results in a tactile
architecture that thrills
the senses.

The use of traditional Malay porches together with Malaccan-style staircases are carefully blended into the main buildings.

The architects believe in the use and adaptation of cross-cultural architectural devices to invoke fresh Southeast Asian images.

The form of the hotel's public buildings and facilities is drawn from a wide variety of Southeast Asian precedents.

Traditional Malay barge-board details can be seen in the gable end treatment.

Opposite: View of distant villas and the verdant backdrop from the main pool.

ocated in the artist's village of Ubud, the Chedi is one of the latest additions to the seemingly unabated spate of resort constructions in Bali. Designed by Kerry Hill, who has consistently garnered some of the most enviable commissions in the region, this building continues the practice's ongoing pursuit of architecturally-engaging functionalism infused with an Asian essence, committed as much to modernity as to local culture.

The Chedi inevitably lends itself to comparisons with two of Kerry Hill's other resort projects in Bali – the three-star Serai at Candi Desa and the canonical Amanusa at Nusa Dua. After the high accolodes that have been showered upon the two earlier properties, critics will scrutinise the Chedi with much greater expectation.

It may be worth noting that the evolution of an architect's oeuvre can be said to be marked by the conflict as well as peril inherent in the duality of confirmation and invention. In every new work, important ideas of the preceding projects must be confirmed, and yet new concepts advanced.

The balance between these twin factors, which is apparent to Hill, is an extremely delicate one. While predictability and repetition are inevitably associated with a bankruptcy of ideas and a degeneration into self-caricature, ever-changing inclinations invariably give the impression of a lack of bearing, perhaps most succintly illustrated by the Miesian aphorism that " one shouldn't invent a new architecture every Monday morning".

In Hill's recent works, past ideas have been more consistently resolved and subtly modulated. One also senses a swerve at this jucture toward an even greater abstraction of both Modernist principles as well as local idioms. Both sources are "appropriated" in a search for

The restaurant pavilion overlooks the expansive valley below.

an "appropriate" and culturally specific interpretation of modernity, recalling the felicitous slogan "appropriate modernity" coined by Chilean critic Cristián Fernández Cox.

All of Hill's three resort projects in Bali employ a reductionist palette that is used to achieve maximum effect. While the guestroom blocks at the Serai are immutably related to the site and to each other in the compositional and spatial sense, those at the Chedi are dispersed in a rather random and repetitious manner, creating a monotonous experiential event. There is also much looseness in the site layout, resulting in a lack of both clarity and a sense of definition in the public spaces. The siting of the public blocks has also not taken advantage of the spectacular setting.

The main reception lobby is a deliberately low-key, single-storey structure with a huge thatched roof simply supported by timber columns or *tiangs*. The detailing throughout the resort is quintessentially minimal. Fully conscious of the dangers of re-casting the design formula that has so far brought him success, Kerry Hill tries to push his blend of functionalism and tradition a little further each time. Here, there are obviously interesting attempts at innovations which have fairly successful results. These are especially apparent in the guestroom blocks where fenestration details employ stonework

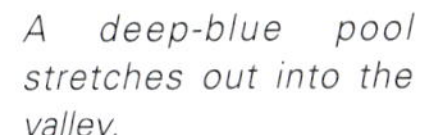

A deep-blue pool stretches out into the valley.

Top: Traditional materials are employed to great effect.

Next page: Guestroom blocks are treated in a quintessentially minimal manner.

to subtle effects. Accommodation includes 28 superior rooms, 28 deluxe rooms, 4 valley suites and 4 village suites.

The Chedi is a suitably dignified and certainly a welcome addition to the resort scene of Ubud. Quibbles aside, this is an immensely civilised building. The lighting at night is especially enchanting, imbuing the place with a special ambience. But perhaps the lack of *élan* is the reason it is unable to evoke the romance inherent in the Balinese landscape.

The edge of the pool dissolves into the distant greenery.

The roof of the restaurant block is simply supported by slender timber posts.

Opposite: Fenestration details are handled in a subtle manner using natural materials.

The Amandari Resort, designed by Australian architect Peter Muller in 1989, is an important precedent in the resort architecture of Southeast Asia. With its series of thatched pavilions located at the picturesque Sayan ridge in Bali, and its famous 'knife-edge' pool, the intimate resort has spawned a number of progeny and its variations. Frequented by trendy jetsetters, the individual pavilion's private outdoor bath flanked by water gardens has also proved to be an enduring model.

In many ways, Amandari has generated an important 'filtering-down' effect by raising the level of architectural consciousness in many new hotels in Bali. Examples of refreshing new hotels that have come onto the Ubud scene, which precisely exemplify the current approach towards hotel architecture in Bali, include Waka di Ume and Ibah.

Ibah, located in Tjampuhan, was completed on the former site of the Tjetjak Inn in 1995. The sense of intimacy in this essentially modest hotel, whose name means 'bequest' in Indonesian, is tangibly evident. Packed within a tight site, the individual pavilions are placed fairly close to one another. As the site is very steep, the pavilions are located on different tiers of varying height. These terraces produce a great sense of horizontality. There is also a sense of

The pool is located at one end of the resort, thus ensuring its privacy.

Top: View of the pool from a high vantage point.

inevitablity in the planning layout. A narrow lane which leads into the site splits the lobby pavilion from the ubiquitous 'knife-edge' pool. Heavy masonry bases anchor the pavilions to the ground while the steeply pitched, thatched roofs provide an elegant sense of lightness. These pavilions overlook tranquil villages and verdant rice fields. The result is an animated setting that evokes a village-like atmosphere.

Like the rest of the resort, the interior of the villas is characterised by a lack of pomposity. Openings are designed in an unaffected manner, with views directed toward the rice fields. On the whole, the use of forms is collage-like and eclectic. Such juxtapostion does give Ibah the quality of organic growth. The landscape is also handled in a seemingly random manner. But the result is surprising and enjoys a refreshing directness, making this cosy resort a favourite among many tourists.

Spacious decks in the villas provide delightful views of the grounds.

The reception lobby is surrounded by water features and dense landscape.

An intimate feel is achieved in the reception lobby through its deliberately casual layout.

Opposite: View of one of the villas located on higher terrain.

Characterised by intense sunshine, heavy rainfall, prevailing winds, high humidity and equable temperatures, climate has always been a prime factor of built forms in Sri Lanka. For years, the architectural scene in the country has been dominated by one outstanding personality – Geoffrey Bawa. Sri Lankan architecture is still largely framed by Bawa's series of exquisite houses and intimate hotels. Many architects in Southeast Asia especially, have been greatly inspired by these seminal works.

However, many contemporary works in Sri Lanka are now being produced by a new generation of architects who have been directly influenced by Bawa, either as co-designers or as a staff in his office. These include architects like C. Anjalendran and Anura Ratnavibhushana. Their culturally sensitive works, although essentially characterised by similar qualities found in Bawa's buildings, sought a new vital expression wholly their own.

In Ratnavibhushana's works, the basic elements are still there. Cool courtyards, fluid interaction between outdoor and indoor spaces, steeply pitched roofs with wide eaves and a concern for shade and cross ventilation are important architectural devices. These buildings, offering immediate and direct contact with the landscape, also respond to local needs and lifestyles with a lively sense of tradition.

Ratnavibhushana's suburban houses are especially noteworthy, offering many lessons for designing climatically sensitive houses in the tropics. Executed with rigorous intensity, the Ariyasinghe House overlooks the huge expanse of Diyawanna Lake where the grand Parliament

Timber posts are supported on cantilevered beams.

Complex designed by Geoffrey Bawa is located. The architect's uncompromising skills have been employed to produce an intimate double-storey detached house, designed with an understated but coherent vocabulary. Within a relatively tight site, the architect manages to design a series of carefully orchestrated spaces that are light, airy and floating.

Bold displays of foliage are carefully framed as part of the views from the interiors. A flat roof terrace was also designed for entertaining. Pastel blue walls form interesting backdrops to staircases and columns. Niches in the walls for holding candles further add to the theatrical quality. Blue-coloured ceilings are also distinctive features of this double-storey detached house.

A square pool at the entrance courtyard

Top and left: The architect has designed a series of carefully orchestrated spaces using the courtyard as a theme.

creates a general feeling of repose. The quality of ever-changing light reflected off the water is especially magical at night. Cross ventilation is encouraged through the minimal use of walls and the liberal use of grilles. Spaces are generally opened to the prevailing breezes. The ambiguous relationship between inside and outside is exploited to provide a thoroughly memorable atmosphere of serenity essential for a family dwelling. Pools, walls and landscape coalesce to bring a sense of tranquillity and lightness.

Ratnavibhushana is indisputably a highly sensitive craftsman of space. His awareness of working in a specific spatial and temporal environment is tangibly evident. The interweaving of building, site and culture offers evidence that an invigorating pursuit of traditional lessons can produce a pleasurable yet relevant contemporary architecture in today's mediocrities of international fashion.

View up the stairwell.

The ambiguous relationship between inside and outside is fully exploited throughout the house.

A blue-hued wall creates a delightful backdrop for the pool.

TRANQUILLITY

"All good architecture which does not express serenity fails in its spiritual vision"

Luis Barragán

Water is commonly used to express a sense of tranquillity.

Opposite: A pervasive calm descends upon this villa at Bintan, Indonesia.

A truly tranquil piece of architecture has a great presence. Another word for this sense of tranquillity is, of course, solitude. As the Mexican poet Octavio Paz asserts : "Solitude is the profundest fact of the human condition." In one of his most important works, *The Labyrinth of Solitude*, Paz passionately argues that "Work, the only modern god, is no longer creative. It is endless, infinite work, corresponding to the inconclusive life of modern society. And the solitude it engenders - the random solitude of hotels, offices, shops and movie theatres - is not a test that strengthens the soul, a necessary purgatory. It is utter damnation, mirroring a world without exit."[1]

In the best of architectural works, the sense of solitude that is inevitably present is one that "strengthens the soul". This sense of solitude, at once affirmative and engaging, makes us aware of our fundamental existence. It is Man's best companion, and it always evokes a moment of silence, one in which the viewer hears only his own heartbeat while contemplating a work of architecture. It allows for reflection of self and contemplation of the work, and is necessary for the disclosure of the poetic moment inherent within architectural objects.

Designed by Bill Bensley, this pool in Bali evokes the ubiquitous sense of serenity present in the Novotel Benoa.

One of the architect's tasks is to open up a view into another reality – one of memories, imagination and dreams. It is one that helps us understand who we are. This is perhaps most aptly illustrated by Noel Arnaund's remark that "I am the space where I am."[2] An architecture of tranquillity silences everything else around it while opening up this view into another reality.

A certain austerity and abstraction characterise works that evoke a sense of tranquillity. Like tectonic mirages in exotic sites of unsurpassed beauty, these sybaritic havens are both theatrical and stage set-like, exuding a blissful serenity and meditative quality. Places like Bali, especially the artists' village of Ubud, is still a place of tremendous serenity. Even in the hustle-bustle of urban environments, architects like Luis Barragán and Tadao Ando have proven that such oases are possible, and indeed both transformative and essential.

It is perhaps the fear of the cacophonous and the momentariness in architecture that prompted the jury for the prestigious 1992 Carlsberg Architectural Prize to pick Ando as the recipient. The jury's citation praises him for : ". . . his reactive nature, his fear of impending chaos, his will to create a haven of calm . . ."

This also reflects the resistance against the disenchanted world of gratuitous imagery. Ando's monumental forms, with their optimistic reassurance of timelessness and a reinterpretation of the past that suggest authenticity, have attracted a huge coterie of serious admirers. The sense of tranquillity in his works, together with their multiple resonances, are spiritually grounded in a mode suggestive of the seminal works of Wright, Aalto and Kahn completed earlier in this century. These inimitable masterworks of the modern tradition have always produced works that set off vibrations associated with calmness, repose and tranquillity – qualities that are increasingly scarce in our frenetic world. They are needed to provide the essential background for contemplative quiescence and the phenomenological experience of inhabiting space.

Centuries ago, the great German philosopher

At the Regent Chiang Mai, lush landscapes create a pervasive air of tranquillity.

Goethe refused to partake in the then fashion-
able art of neurotic rhetoric. He reacted against
the prevailing chaos by producing literary works
of ordered logic and lucid clarity. He advised
painters to dip their brushes in reason and
architects to aim at noble simplicity. In the end,
all architects' works are evaluated on the
significance of the experience their architecture
provides – the lived reality of their buildings. This
has absolutely nothing to do with the hysterical
search for the new, nor with the use of
gratuitous imagery. We require simple places
to live and work, but places that can also truly
be the most sublime stage sets for human
drama. For that to happen, an architecture of
tranquillity must exist.

In his address upon receipt of the Pritzker Prize
for Architecture in 1980, Luis Barragán asserts
that "I have always tried to allow for the interior placid murmur of silence, and in my
fountains, silence sings." For him, serenity is
"the great and true antidote against anguish and
fear. Today, more than ever, it is the architect's
duty to make of it a permanent guest in the
home, no matter how sumptuous or how humble. Throughout my work I have always strived
to achieve serenity, but one must be on guard
not to destroy it by the use of an indiscriminate
palette."

Footnotes:

1   Octavio Paz, *The Labyrinth of Solitude*, Grove
Press, Inc., 1961, p. 204

2   Quoted in Gaston Bachelard, *Poetics of Space*, pp.131

Tranquillity reigns in this garden at Villa Bebek, Bali.

Top right: Traditional Thai structures are built over water bodies.

Bottom right: Paradise Island Resort, Maldives.

A private bath overlooks an enclosed courtyard.

The aquamarine blue expanse of the sea at Ko Samui, Thailand.

Opposite: Pool at Banyan Tree Bintan, Indonesia.

A restrained palette of materials is employed to create spaces of great repose.

Infusing rationality with the expressive potency of light and space, this delightful house is conceptualised by Singapore-based designer Juan Peck Foon of Resources+Planning Design Consultants. Blending a refreshing solution with a practical reality, this light-filled scheme has been carefully designed to uphold the clean-cut design philopsophy of the practice.

The genesis of the house is in response to site conditions. Marked by an apparent modesty, materials and detailing are essentially simple. While many other newly renovated houses in the same neighbourhood are exercises in pomposity, this house asserts an air of unadorned simplicity. Adjectives that immediately come to mind when discussing this house include serene, gentle and subtle.

The main architectural preoccupations are with space and light. The subtle play of light and volume, especially in the living room, asserts an air of meditative power. The high volume space and its extension to the outdoors make this public area the focus of the design.

Juan's masterly handling of a restrained palette of materials is also evident. Several spatial moves, made within a relatively tight budget but with unflagging rigour, prove that simplicity can be both stunning and practical. Spaces overlap and frame vistas. The house engages on a highly visceral level. For all its simplicity of construction and studied minimalism, the house is a delight to experience. Although the designer's palette is rigorous, there is a spirit of refined intensity.

Subtle play of light and
volume asserts an air of
meditative power.

Planes are used to create a sense of both spatial division as well as visual linkage.

Opposite: High volume spaces make the house a delight to experience.

Small touches enliven the sobriety of the design.

Banyan Tree Bintan, a new resort operated by Banyan Tree Hotels and Resorts and developed by Tropical Resorts Ltd, is the fourth Banyan Tree Resort.

Located on a bay at Tanjong Said on Bintan Islands, on a 240 - hectare elevated seafront site with a commanding view, Banyan Tree Bintan is only 45 kilometres south of Singapore. Designed by Architrave Design and Planning, Phase I of the resort comprises 27 villas modelled on traditional Balinese architecture. An addditional 13 villas and a 200 - room low-rise five-star hotel are scheduled to be added in the near future.

Villas, supported by massive concrete stilts, are perched on hill slopes set amid lush landscapes facing the sea. There are three Pool Villas of 391 square metres each and 24 Jacuzzi Villas of 133 square metres each. The former has two bedrooms with attached bathrooms, a living room and a private pool while the latter has a bedroom with attached bathroom, a living room and an open-air jacuzzi.

Suffused with an intense tranquillity, the picturesque landscape creates a verdant beauty of immense vitality. Every view in the resort is directed towards the wide expanse of sky and sea. Tucked against the hillside, the ensemble is stage-like. Twilight casts a special spell.

Environmental sensitivity has been fundamen-

The Pool Villa has two bedrooms flanking a private pool.

tal to Banyan Tree's concept and development approach. The resort, set within untouched forests where trees are as old as 80 -100 years, is amazingly tranquil. To ensure their preservation, the villas are designed around most of these trees. These villas are all finished with traditional Balinese materials like lava stone, granite marble and thatched roofs.

In the final analysis, the project is greatly informed by a sense of respect for the fragile environment. Of course, the use of Balinese elements to invoke a cultural sensibility in the context of Bintan is highly questionable. Although the architecture is not particularly original in its conception, it nevertheless exudes a general feeling of order and repose in a unique setting.

Every view is directed towards the sea.

Villas are supported by concrete stilts.

Top & bottom: Views of the Pool Villa.

The circular pool is fringed by tall, existing trees.

Opposite: At twilight, the resort is suffused with an intense spell of great repose.

At sunset, the resort is suffused with an intense spell
of great repose.

ocated in the highly commercialised district of Nusa Dua in Bali, this is a golf-oriented villa development planned in conjunction with the adjacent resort hotel of Amanusa. Currently, three model villas have been built. The landscape is also well established.

The architect for these villas is Kerry Hill Architects, whose works are distinguished by the creative use of local resources and means of production. The practice's attempts at appropriating the language of architec-

View of the overall land-scape.

tural modernity in local terms, and with cultured discipline, have been convincing. Many earlier projects, like the Datai in Malaysia and Amanusa, have helped to redirect the discourse on regional identity toward the notion of an "appropriated" modernity.

Set within huge compounds, each villa comprises several pavilions grouped around landscaped gardens. Skilful handling of scale and proportion is obvious. A rich sequence of spatial and material manipulation is evident, while a scrupulous simplicity pervades the design. There is a total absence of fuss. The no-fudge approach, a trademark of the architect, is carried through with great discipline.

Designed along traditional Balinese lines, the individual pavilions create a casual setting for the residents and their guests. All areas are open to the breezes. They are protected from the elements by bamboo blinds or sliding panels. The pavilions' most outstanding quality is the way spaces flow from the indoors to the outdoor, while blending intangible qualities of the tropics into a delightful mix.

The interiors, conceived by Jaya Ibrahim, also share the same frugality of materials, although they lack the sensuality of the designer's earlier works. The sensitive placement of the various pavilions has created a strongly introspective setting within a relatively bland and feature-less site. Although the design has not broken new grounds, the architect's laconic conception has produced a series of private villas that exudes a great sense of tranquillity. On the whole, it is a design that truly celebrates tropical living.

Open-sided pavilions are a common feature of every villa.

View towards the pool.

A pool pavilion is set amid the hard and soft landscapes.

Previous page: The villas, sited in an apparently random manner, have a high level of privacy through the sensitive use of walls.

An introspective setting is created with the help of land-scaped pools and lush plants.

Opposite: A scrupulous simplicity pervades the design.

The relatively small house is set within a dense landscape of great intimacy.

Located in the traffic-choked environment of Bangkok in Thailand, this private residence is situated in the suburban residential district of Soi Chang Ket, off Sukhumvit Road. Traditional timber houses in Bangkok have virtually been wiped out of existence and replaced by largely bland and ill-conceived steel-and-glass towers. Hence it is both a surprise and a delight to find the Bensley Residence in such a context. The two-pavilion house was designed by the owner, landscape architect Bill Bensley of Bensley Design Group. Based in Bangkok, Bensley is well-known for the design of some highly exquisite gardens in various parts of Asia. Designing tropical gardens as a series of vignettes or individual stories, Bensley's approach can best be summed up by his declaration that "beauty is created when there is no clear, expected boundary. Tropical architecture should embrace the landscape, and invite it into its deepest rooms."

This approach is clearly extended to the design of his own residence. Set amid a lushly landscaped and intimate garden, the house is a tranquil private world where the ambience of serenity is totally pervasive. A bold display of luminous foliage confronts the visitor upon entering the wall-enclosed compound. Sensitive landscaping, combined with found and sculpted artefacts, makes the essentially small compound seem much larger. The impact of the tropical idyll is almost immediate. A well-crafted timber staircase leads up to two traditional Thai pavilions originally from Ayutthaya. Perfectly proportioned, they were acquired by Thai architect Saichol Saejew and reassembled to form two richly evocative garden courtyards.

Remodelled to suit contemporary living, these two pavilions are linked by an open-air timber deck on the second level. Serving as the main living space, this deck is probably the most important and delightful part of the house. It truly demonstrates that although the primary function of a house is shelter, its richness is derived from the simultaneous experience of the interior and the exterior. Bensley has cleverly exploited these open-to-sky spaces as important features throughout the house, linking all enclosed rooms.

On the second level, each pavilion accommodates one small but comfortable bedroom with an attached bathroom. A dining room is located beneath one of the pavilions, while the space beneath the other pavilion houses a kitchen, maids' quarters and a small gymnasium. The picturesque high gable ends of the roofs are closed off by the distinctive design of the barge board, the most poignant symbol of Thai architecture.

Monochromatic interior finishes also utilise local materials to great effect, evoking a highly languorous and tranquil feel. In its modest way, the house invigorates and re-engages more of our senses by using visual, tactile and auditory cues in new, refreshing ways. On a relatively small plot of land, the Bensley Residence exudes expansiveness and delight. Above all, it evinces a sense of serenity everywhere

An outdoor dining spot is carefully marked out by hard landscape.

The mood of the house is especially enchanting in the evening, when careful placement of lighting brings out the subtleties of traditional Thai design.

Opposite: The living room is located on the ground level of one of the pavilions.

TRANSPARENCY

"And now here is my secret, a very simple secret: It is only with the heart that one can see rightly; What is essential is invisible to the eye."

Antoine de Saint-Exupéry

A sense of transparency suggests an expanse that lies beyond.

Opposite: This house at Bishopsgate, Singapore, allows for a simultaneous perception of different spatial locations.

Dematerialisation of the solid can be expressed in many ways.

T he modernist concept of transparency refers to the use of transparent materials like glass to achieve demarcations in a spatial continuum. But in the traditional architecture of Southeast Asia, dematerialisation of the solid is expressed in many ways. The important sense of transparency can be achieved through the deliberate placement of structures, openings and screens. Many of them engage through recurring themes of spatial layering. Spaces are layered to indicate degrees of formality or ceremony, yet linked in a visually compelling manner.

The most obvious example is the traditional Thai house, where door and window openings are often detailed with shutters that allow views into other parts of the common terrace. Permeable walls and screens also demarcate different spaces while allowing a sense of transparency. Space can be inflected, manipulated and articulated by planes, openings and columns. In Balinese architecture, the grouping of pavilions within compounds also allow views through a series of layered outdoor and indoor spaces.

Buildings are not simply hermetic containers of space. Architecture can be perceived as an inhabited art - a space-making activity in light, where the solid has always been the servant of the void. This void is manifested through layered spaces, which form an important part of the tropic consciousness. They allow for a simultaneous perception of other spatial boundaries, evoking realms that are different yet sharing a common macrocosm.

In traditional buildings, such transparency is achieved without eschewing privacy and enclosure. Screens are treated as interposing elements that accentuate distance and differ-

In this house in Bali designed by Michael White, demarcations in a spatial continuum are ambiguously defined by positions of columns, roof lines and landscape features.

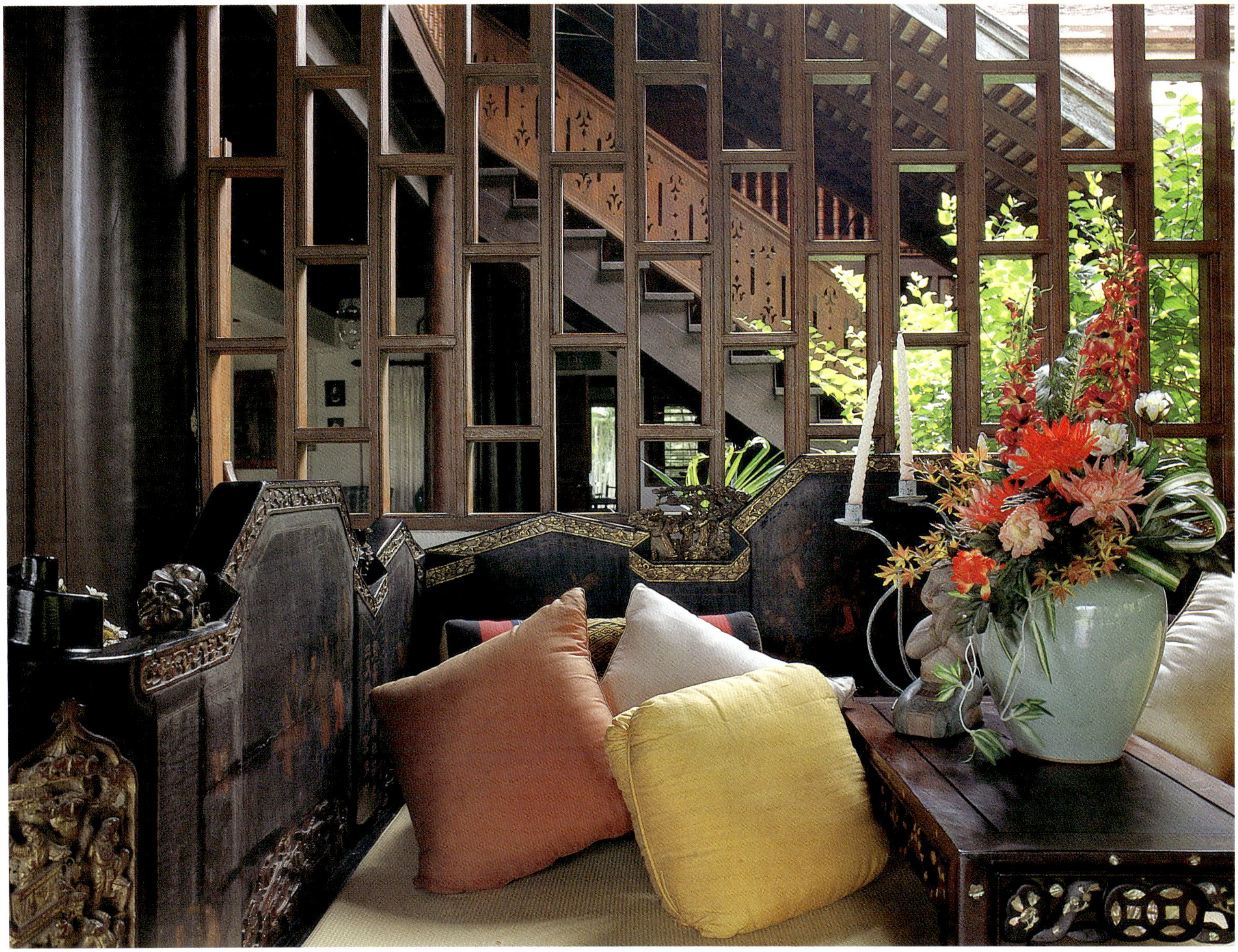

Screens can be used as interposing elements that accentuate distance and difference.

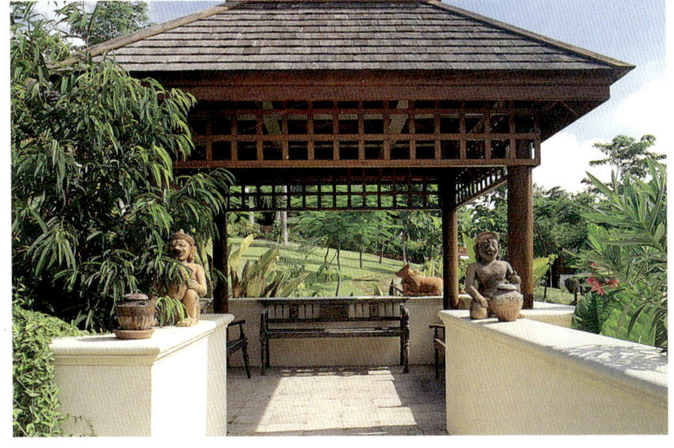

Recurring themes of spatial layering, like the use of pavilions to stop a visual axis, are found in the traditional architecture of the region.

ence. A sense of transparency is not simply one that reveals everything. Rather, it suggests an expanse that lies beyond. Space can be manipulated to be expanding and dynamic or controlled and static. Confronted with a continuous unfolding of changing perspectives, the viewer experiences the pleasures of containment and revelation.

Colin Rowe termed this effect 'phenomenal transparency', defining it in Georgy Kepes' words: "If one sees two or more figures overlapping one another, and each of them claims for itself the common overlapped part, then one is confronted with a contradiction of spatial dimensions. To resolve this contradiction, one must assume the presence of a new optical quality. The figures are endowed with transparency: that is, they are able to interpenetrate without an optical destruction of each other. Transparency however implies more than an optical characteristic, it implies a broader spatial order. Transparency means a simultaneous perception of different spatial locations. Space not only recedes but fluctuates in a continuous activity."[1]

Footnotes:

1   Quoted in Colin Rowe, *The Mathematics of the Ideal Villa and Other Essays*, pp. 160

In contemporary structures, glass is commonly used to achieve spatial demarcation.

Opposite: Permeable walls, screens and windows demarcate spaces while allowing a sense of transparency.

Left & right: In traditional buildings, spaces are layered to indicate degrees of formality or ceremony, yet linked in a visually compelling manner.

At the Serai in Bali, open-sided walkways allow views through a series of layered outdoor and indoor spaces.

A well-lit courtyard forms the focus of the house.

Centre: The use of the courtyard as the main visual element allows the house to achieve a great sense of transparency.

Sir Stamford Raffles, in his Town Plan of Singapore in 1822, had allowed for a linear arrangement of shophouses of specified widths linked by a colonnaded '5-foot' walkway. Subsequently influenced by the needs of the local populace, the built-form that emerged was also a response to the tropical climate.

The typical features of a shophouse include brick walls with high ceilings, roofs with secondary jack-roofs to allow hot air to escape, an airwell to provide light and ventilation, and a shop-front at the first storey for the occupants to ply their trades. The early prototypes of these buildings were purely utilitarian structures, and it was only in the early 1900s that elaborate architectural motifs from European, Malay and Chinese architecture were introduced in an ornamental and unrestrained manner to the front facades.

Although the conservation and restoration of areas rich in historic architecture is essential in providing tangible links to Singapore's heritage, the allure of shophouses as an alternative housing type is probably due to their limited numbers. However, the "yuppified" status of shophouses generally attract owners and architects who do appreciate the unique spatial qualities inherently present in these structures. One of such shophouses, designed by architect Richard Ho, is located in the Blair Road Conservation Area.

The shophouse has been gutted and given a new lease of life through clever manipulation of planes and vertical elements. The external fabric, including the front elevation and rear extension, remains intact because of the authorities' imposed guidelines. Internally, it was however radically re-configured.

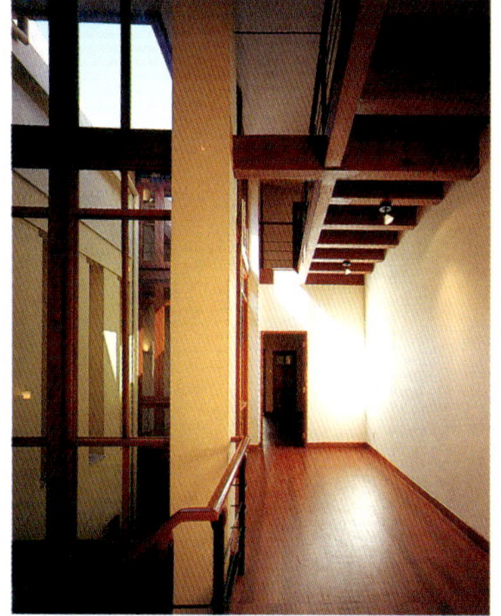

Spaces are layered in an intricate manner by the careful placement of walls, openings and various partitions. The focus of the internal space is a lightwell, which acts as an important pivotal point in the house. It is also the most dramatic part of the design, providing soft, diffused natural light to the three floors. The sense of transparency is obvious, imbuing the house with a general feeling of openness.

The public spaces are located on the first storey. The staircase leading to the private spaces above forms the main feature of the space. The entire vertical circulation route revolves around the lightwell, which is a simple but effective means of creating spatial delight.

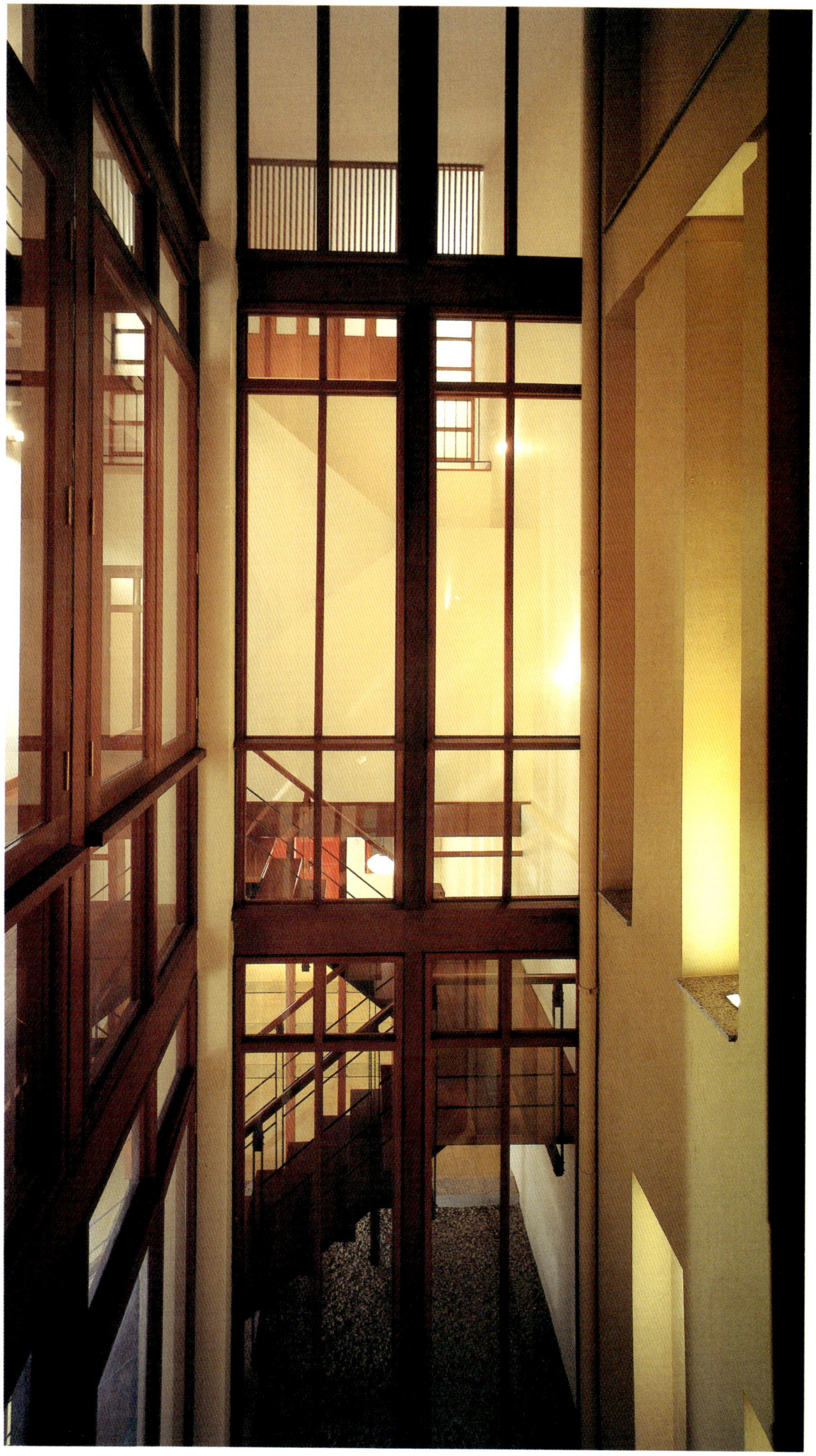

View of the staircase through a series of glass planes.

The triumph is its discipline and total lack of contrivance — the architect doing only what is essential in creating an internal environment that is functional and delightful without resorting to nostalgia for an imagined lifestyle and ornamentation found in many other conserved shophouses.

Without doubt, the humble and essentially utilitarian shophouse continues to provide a constant source of inspiration to new contemporary designs. However, they are certainly not monuments to be either replicated or preserved. Tradition is an evolving, as opposed to static, notion. To create a richer future, we must neither embalm nor replicate the past. The challenge in conservation lies in steering a delicate course between maintaining the essence of traditional forms and accommodating new spatial and functional dimensions that are essential in a dynamic society.

Space is carefully manipulated to provide a continuous unfolding of changing perspectives.

Opposite: Spatial layering is achieved through the careful placement of different architectural elements.

Most people erroneously associate tropical architecture with pitched roofs. But tropical architecture is not a style; and as such, it has no physical characteristics. It is about responding to the climate in ways that would enhance the quality of space.

The 'in-between' realm, the indeterminate zone between outside and inside, is surely one of the most pleasant spaces in any house. Most houses are unfortunately mere boxes designed with total disregard for the importance of these spaces.

A recently completed detached house in Serangoon Gardens, designed by Juan Peck Foon, demonstrates that a truly tropical house needs no pitched roof. At the same time, it is a house that revolves around enclosed gardens and a private courtyard, offering many delightful 'in-between' spaces.

The rectilinear house, located on an almost square piece of land of 4,500 sq ft, has none of the decorative trivialities of Neo-Classicism. To suit a contemporary lifestyle, the house is tailored precisely to the specific demands and pragmatic concerns of the clients who are a young couple with two children. The upper floor, which houses the master bedroom, was set back in order to provide a sense of continuity with the neighbours. This set-back not only buffers the bedroom from the road, but also creates a serene courtyard in the middle of the house.

On the first storey, the living and dining areas are located on one side of the pebbled court-yard, while three other bedrooms situated on the other side also overlook this tranquil space. All these rectilinear spaces have a great sense of repose, especially the courtyard, which has a strong meditative calmness.

A circulation path runs around the courtyard. The configuration of the spaces facilitate cross ventilation, making the house comfortable without the need for air-conditioning. There is also a pool along the length of the living room, providing a delightful complement to the space. The kitchen, which is located towards the end of the living room, also enjoys a view of the pool. Throughout, there is a simultaneous perception of different spatial locations

View of the children's room into the courtyard and the living room beyond.

Front elevation of the house at night.

Juan's consistent and steadfast approach is clearly evident. Walls are simply plastered and painted while floors are finished with terracotta tiles. Chengal timber is used for doors and windows. The articulation of architectural elements like columns and beams is simple but neat. The designer minimises unnecessary junctions and controls positions of beams, columns, slabs and bathroom location so that false ceiling is dispensed with.

All built-in and several loose furniture pieces are custom-designed as integral parts of the house. The result is a sensitively considered scheme which infuses a simple dwelling with surprising elegance and spatial expansiveness. But more importantly, it is a rare demonstration that tropical living is about the enrichment of the delightful 'in-between' realm.

The kitchen is directly connected to the living and dining rooms.

A cantilevered roof plane
hovers above the en-
trance driveway.

Glass and openings are used to achieve a strong sense of transparency.

A lush lotus pond forms the foreground to one of the villas.

Designed as a private residence, the grandeur of this complex of individual pavilions is probably the strongest intial impression for any visitor. Situated at Tanah Gajah, east of Ubud, this extended family compound is built over a period of 15 years.

Conceptualised by the owner, Hendra Hadiprana, a respected authority on Javanese and Balinese architecture, the pavilions are designed for his family and guests. Set amid rice fields, the sense of serenity is absolute. The main reception pavilion, or *bale gede* is the first structure that one encounters upon arival. Open-sided, it is linked to the dining pavilion which overlooks a rectangular swimming pool.

With the assistance of architect Faried Masdoeki, the overall design principles are inspired by traditional Balinese and Javanese architecture. The articulation of hierarchical orders is subtle, yet manages to mark the complex's formal presence in the landscape. Pavilions are laid out on various axes, creating a sense of ceremony and giving the place a grand unity of composition. Tiles, rather than the traditional Balinese thatch or *alang-alang*, are used for the roofs. Although the form is Balinese, there is a certain sense of eclecticism, brought about by the owner's deployment of both Javanese and Balinese elements.

The pool pavilion is directly linked to the villa by a covered walkway.

The landscaping, unlike the more popular Balinese style of dense gardens, is sensitively controlled to give careful framing of views and to create a delighful complement to the pavilions. The expansiveness of the landscape is further exploited by the use of water features that act as landscape dividers between the pavilions. To meander through the site is to experience an interesting series of perspectives as the estate reveals itself slowly. The place is especially enchanting at night. Subtle lighting highlights each building while a whole cacophony of sounds from the embracing nature is complemented by the gurgle of streams and water features. The wonderful sense of tranquillity is perhaps the estate's most outstanding quality.

Sculptural objects provide a spatial marker for this huge reflecting pool.

View of the reception pavilion.

Sculpted objects can be found throughout the complex.

The articulation of hierarchical orders is subtle, yet manages to mark the complex's formal presence in the landscape.

This open-sided pavilion is the latest addition to the ever-evolving complex.

Opposite: Transitional spaces link the various pavilions and amenities in a seamless manner.

View of the entrance path from the reception pavilion.

A pool outside one of the smaller villas.

Interior of the reception pavilion.

Pathway leading to other villas.

In this recently completed house at Bishopsgate, Singapore, designed by Chan Soo Khian of SCDA in collaboration with Architects 61, spaces are treated with a poetic intensity. It is urban in location, yet rural in spirit. In general the 6,000 sq ft house inspires feelings of great repose. The preference for elemental architectural expression is evident. An allusive vocabulary of forms is manifested through beguiling simplicity.

Roofs are designed to "float" above the ceilings in an attempt to imbue a sense of lightness to the structures. Its richly intimate rooms, all directed towards lush gardens and water courts, engender a disarming sense of engagement with the elements.

Designed around a two-tier pool consisting of a landscaped pool and a swimming pool, the house is truly a sanctuary of uninvaded calm. The interplay of landscape and architecture creates a place that is full of unfolding vistas. Framed openings and layered planes lead the viewer's eye in the most revealing route.

In the words of Geoffrey Bawa: "a building can only be understood by moving around and through it and by experiencing the modulation and feel of the spaces one moves through..." This house succintly demonstrates a concern to distil essentials. It evokes the sense of stasis and movement, security and vulnerability, outdoors and indoors – qualities which encapsulate buildings in the tropics.

View of the pool from the entrance pavilion.

Courtyards punctuate the various spaces.

The landscaped pool is visually linked with the swimming pool.

Interior view of the living room.

Right: Night view of the house from the garden.

AMBIGUITY

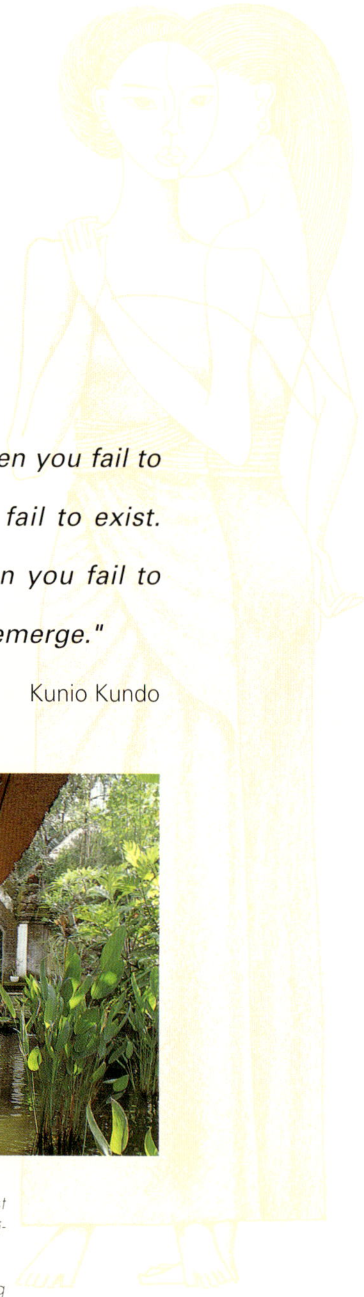

"In the West, when you fail to describe, things fail to exist. In the East, when you fail to describe, things emerge."

Kunio Kundo

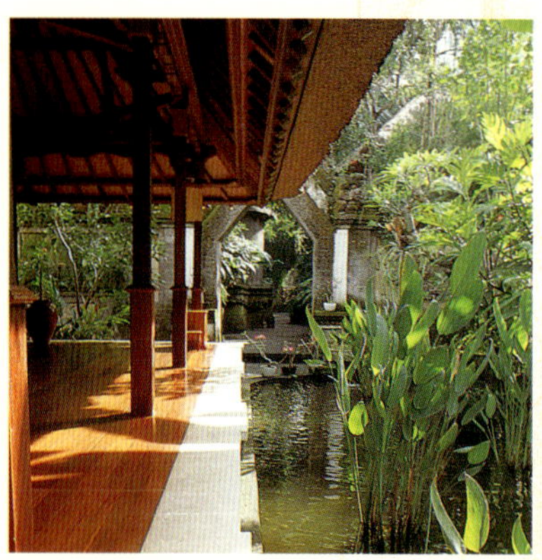

Ambiguity is perhaps best expressed by the indeterminate "in-between" realm.

Opposite: The Regent Chiang Mai, Thailand.

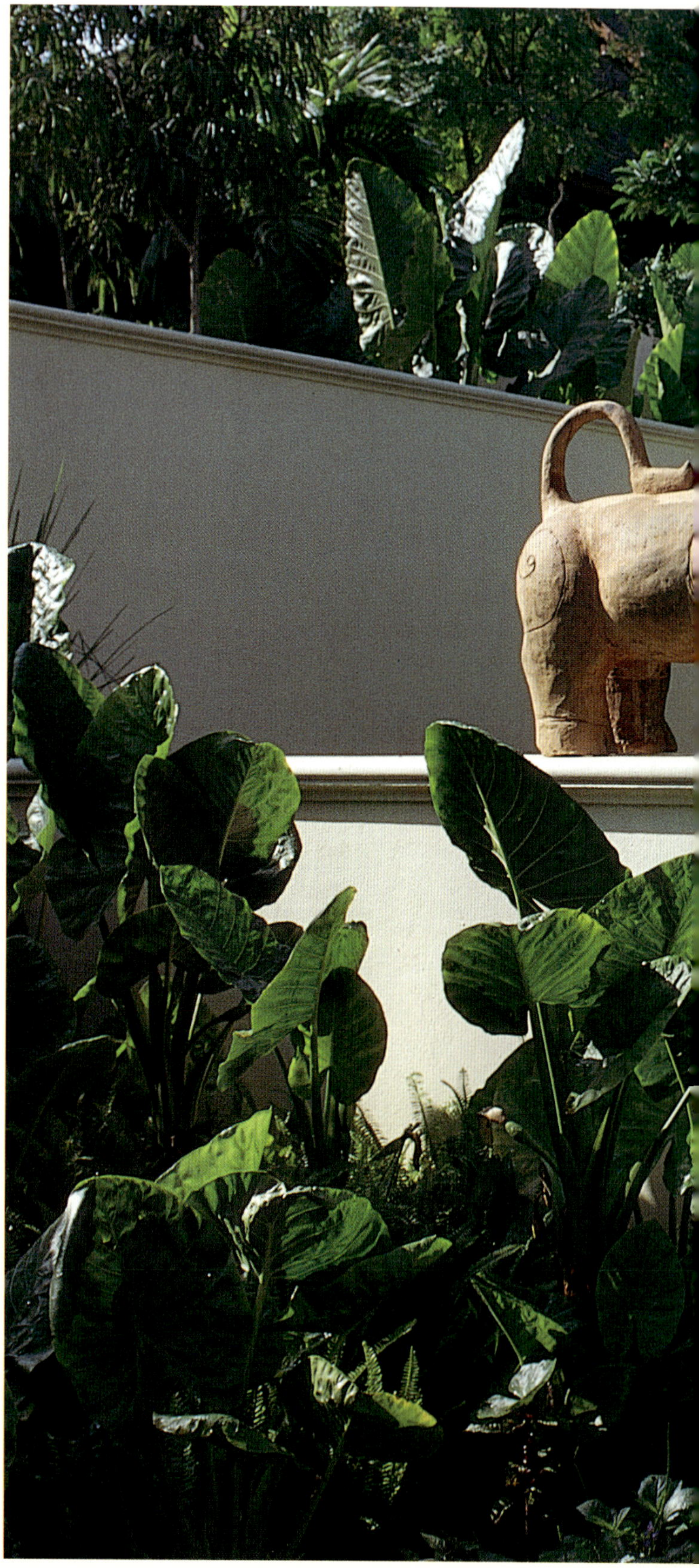

Nusa Dua Beach Hotel, Bali.

There is perhaps no contemporary architect who has responded more profoundly to the notion of ambiguity than the Dutch master Aldo van Eyck. He has articulated a number of insights on what he meant by "twin-phenomena" : " . . . such as open-closed, inside-outside, old-new, often brought up here with others like large-small, many-few, far-near, light-dark, unity-diversity, single-plural, part-whole, similar-dissimilar, rest-movement, order-chaos, space-matter, individual-collective, form a vast network of meaning from which nothing can be lifted . . . All twin phenomenon together form the changing fabric of this network – and the constituent ingredients of architecture. Though different, each of them, they are at the same time – this is the point – also reciprocally open to each other. Far from being mutually exclusive or independent, they merge, lean on each other."[1]

Such a delicate balance of seemingly opposite qualities adds immeasurably to the experiential richness. Van Eyck proceeds to argue that these divergent relationship of parts are in fact complementary and not contradictory. The value of multiple meanings and spatial ambiguity is thus seen as an essential dimension of architecture.

The richness of a building in the tropics is really derived from the constant phenomenological awareness of the interior and the exterior. Tropical living actually occurs here. Such an 'in-between realm' – the ambiguous edge between inside and out, private and public, shadow and light – is intrinsic to the tropic consciousness. Thus, to a greater degree perhaps than in other geographical belts, the in-between realm has always been a critical element in the vocabulary of spatial forms in most parts of Asia.

Villa Bebek, Bali.

The richness of a building in the tropics is derived from the ambiguous edge between outside and inside.

This was delicately illustrated in the Vietnamese movie *The Scent of Green Papaya* Although filmed inside a studio, director Hung Tran Anh's evocative stage set underscores the sensual and associative potential as well as poignancy of such layered and amorphous spaces. These indeterminate zones of enclosure are intrinsic not only to traditional Vietnamese architecture, but are also prevalent in the traditional architecture of Asia. In Thailand, for example, the open-sided gazebo, or *sala*, facilitates outdoor living whilst helping to integrate the exteriors with the interiors.

Filtering and transitional elements, like walls, gateways, steps and thresholds, are delightful architectural elements found in the rich traditional architecture of the region. Handled with grace, they offer much ambiguity and help to create spatial variety. Spaces flow from the interiors to the exteriors in an almost seamless manner, creating interesting intermediate thresholds. In modern architecture, one recalls the works of Alvar Aalto, whose theory of an 'elaborate network of touch' focuses on the articulation of thresholds and zones within a building.

The quality of ambiguity also extends to the effects of various moods. In tropical landscape, one of the most intriguing elements is its ability to conjure different moods at different times of the day. Roberto Burle Marx, the noted Brazilian landscape architect, once remarked that a garden must be created in such a manner that it can be seen in different hours and even in different moods. The beauty of the garden thus lies in its ambiguity and instability.

Footnotes:

1   Aldo van Eyck, quoted in Herman Hertzbeger, *Aldo van Eyck*, Stichting Wonen, Amsterdam, 1982, pp. 43

Patios and terraces bring the outdoors into the house.

Strips of landscaped pools merge with covered walkways in an ambiguous setting of outdoors and indoors.

Opposite: This courtyard provides an ambiguous edge to the house.

Dusit Santiburi, Ko Samui.
Bottom: The Serai, Bali.

ocated at Jalan Jambu Ayer, this domestic retreat of ambiguous spaces was remodelled by Chan Soo Khian of SCDA. On a slightly odd-shaped site of approximately 6,000 sq ft, the designer has chosen to simply open up the existing house with great planning economy. Single-storey pavilions and view courts are then added to take advantage of the grounds and heighten the relationship between indoors and outdoors. These include the car porch, breakfast pavilion and a pool pavilion.

The pivot of the new scheme is obviously the blue-tiled pool located at the eastern corner of the site. This is linked to the pool pavilion which is also connected to the living room. A break-fast pavilion opens out from the kitchen and overlooks lush gardens. Inside, the designer's pleasure in materials and sense of the outdoors are evident. It is both dignified and functional. The master bedroom, located on the first storey, has its own garden courtyard and an outdoor bath and shower. The series of pavilions, finished in honed sandstone, celebrates informality and comfort. They also provide an intermixing of the public and private realms.

The house is a celebration of space through calm suavity. Its splendidly peaceful atmosphere is also a result of an inspired use of elements from Balinese culture. This is an accomplished piece of work combining formal rigour with elegant formality.

A pavilion overlooks the pool and garden.

Night view across the pool into the living room.

Semi-outdoor spaces are present throughout the house.

An outdoor bath shaded by a pergola.

View of the pool from the living room.

One of the bedrooms overlooks an enclosed garden.

The interiors combine formal rigour with elegant formality.

Located in the village of San Pe Sear, on the outskirts of verdant Chiang Mai, this residence is designed by Thai architect Chulathat Kitibutr. Life in this tranquil setting is simple and slow-paced. Known as Baan Ta which means "House by the River Port", the house is placed delicately at the edge of a small river.

The single-storey structure consists of three linked pavilions enclosing a timber-decked courtyard in a horseshoe-shaped composition that overlooks the placid waters of the river. An open-sided pavilion or *sala* sits on the bank of the river. This is often used as a quiet, contemplative spot for meals, accompanied by the delicate rustle of leaves when frequent zephyrs move through the compound.

In the middle of the well-shaded courtyard is a small rectangular pool flanked by a spacious living and dining pavilion on one side, and a bedroom pavilion on the other side. The house, which actually serves as a guesthouse for the owner, has an air of rustic charm and complete isolation. As there are no other houses in its immediate vicinity, the languid river forms a powerful backdrop.

Kitibutr used his knowledge and understanding of Lanna's traditions to delicate effects. Completed about three years ago, the open and uncluttered house is based on traditional Lanna-style architecture. Most of the house is constructed of teak. It is a crisply honed synthesis of solids and voids that achieves an admirable sense of the outdoors without sacrificing functional priorities. More than anything, perhaps, the uneffacingly simple house effectively fulfils the architect's exhortation to create 'an ambiguous blend of outdoor and indoor spaces'.

View of the living room.

Top: A small pool sits in the middle of the compound.

The uneffacingly simple river-side pavilion hovers above the water surface.

Top & bottom: The house has an air of rustic charm and complete isolation.

Opposite: The pool is flanked by the living room and the bedroom pavilion.

Restaurant block.

The Nusa Dua Beach Hotel, one of the early mega-resorts in Bali, was recently refurbished at a cost of US$22 million to "restore the hotel to its original authentic Balinese palace-style design".

The hotel was first opened in 1982, becoming Nusa Dua's first five-star landmark property. The main focus of the new transformation was the hotel's 380 guestrooms and suites. Like most other hotel refurbishment programmes, the bathroom facilities were enlarged while the decor theme focuses on ethnic themes.

Designed by Peddle Thorp Architects from Australia, together with Parama Loka of Jakarta, all areas of the hotel were rejuvenated to reflect a stronger "Balinese character" with the deployment of wooden hues and carefully selected fabric and handicrafts. A wide range of additional facilities, including a Spa & Health Centre complete with a lap pool and spa cafe, a new lagoon-style swimming pool and 5,000 square metres of newly landscaped gardens were added to further enhance the overall ambience of the hotel's grounds.

Pragmatically, the refurbished hotel responds to the exigencies of a brief that attempts to keep in touch with new developments in the resort industry. But architecturally, the project offers few surprises. The only exception is probably the Spa & Health Centre.

This building is the most prominent new feature. Its unique high-volume structure, located to the left of the hotel's entrance driveway, exudes an ascetic refinement wholly its own. Contained within this space are plunge pools, aromatic saunas, cool dips and steam baths. Its outdoor lap pool is set amid a compact, lushly landscaped plot of enclosed courtyard. The feeling evoked is one of delightful ambiguity.

New shading devices are installed in many parts of the renovated hotel.

Next page: The pool at the Spa Centre is enclosed within a lush garden setting.

Pool at the Spa & Health Centre.

Entrance to the Spa Centre.

Geoffrey Bawa is regarded by many outside Sri Lanka as the country's quintessential architect. His lyrical understanding of space and climate is distilled in the essence of all his works, which are profoundly evocative of tradition. The large corpus of Bawa's works, despite being much imitated, remains enticing and durable. His buildings are all very simple and understated. However, the manipulation of light and space demonstrates a rare architectural perception.

Bawa's latest tourist hotel, sited in the untouched rainforests of central Sri Lanka, marks a radical departure from his vocabulary of forms and palette of materials. The crisply tectonic assemblage of the Kandalama Hotel is a great surprise for architectural cognoscenti. Instead of using the ubiquitous pitched roof imagery, Bawa employs an almost Miesian vocabulary of black frames, planar elements and flat roofs.

The most interesting aspect of the design is that Bawa sensitively combines a modernist sensibility with traditional influences. It is apparent that Bawa has intentionally imbued the hotel with a unique exterior that aspires to a state of eventual ruination. The precise tectonic form has been designed to be overtaken by the ravages of time. Vegetation grows from every level of the hotel. This tension between nature and the man-made is made so much more tangible by the deliberate juxtaposition of both elements everywhere in the 150-room hotel. For example, anodised aluminium is used next to raw timber while polished granite is interspersed with rough-hewn rocks.

Environmental issues were the major concerns during the planning stage of the design. Fierce debates raged over the suitability of the fragile site for a tourist development. In the end, extended enviromental impact assessement were carried out before the Government was convinced.

Besides having its own sewerage treatment and disposal plant, the hotel also has deep wells and waste water treatment plant. Hence, the blending of the hotel and the landscape is no

A reflecting pool at roof level.

The main pool overlooks the expansive landscape.

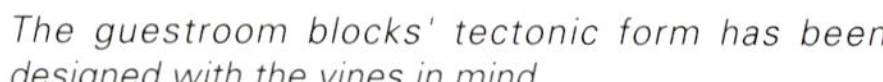

The guestroom blocks' tectonic form has been designed with the vines in mind.

View of the pool.

accident. Created with an exemplary understanding of site and climate, the organic layout sets up an unpredictable rhythm that is arguably one of the design's strongest features. Throughout, the guest is in constant contact with the wonderful panorama of nature.

However the workmanship leaves much to be desired. The interior's discreet formality also evokes a certain coldness that is absent in Bawa's earlier hotels. Quibbles aside, the hotel has been brilliantly conceived and demonstrates Bawa's concern for simplicity and sensitivity in the deployment of materials and resources.

Lift lobbies open into informal lounge areas.

The interiors are sparsely fitted out.

SHADOWS

"Like the musician's breath in a wind instrument, light and shadow bring out the rich qualities of materials, qualities that remain silent in darkness."

Steven Holl

Screens provide an interesting silhouette to openings.

Opposite: In this house at Bishopsgate, Singapore, the effect of light and shadow is created by the deliberate placement of light sources.

Climate affects the form of the environment in a very noticeable manner. Every shelter responds to man's needs for air, light and protection. In the tropics, shading is a fundamental design strategy for preventing excessive heat build-up, for comfort as well as for diffusing sunlight. Hence, it is an important modifying force.

At the same time, Eastern architecture has always had a strong affinity with under-lit interiors and the play of shadows. From the shadowy world of Japanese domestic architecture to the exquisite shadow play of Javanese puppets, the manipulation of light and shadow is an important aspect of the aesthetic tradition.

In his eloquent essay of 1933/34, *In Praise of Shadows*, the famous Japanese writer Jun'ichiro Tanizaki succintly captures the important role of shadows in Japanese sensibility : "The quality that we call beauty, however, must always grow from the realities of life, and our ancestors, forced to live in dark rooms, presently came to discover beauty in shadows, ultimately to guide shadows towards beauty's ends. And so it has come to be that the beauty of a Japanese room depends on a variation of shadows, heavy shadows against light shadows – it has nothing else." [1]

The poetic fusion of light and space has been considered one of the basic tenets of architecture. In the East, this is extended to the richness of effect created by the changing permeations of light caused by the constantly moving trajectory of the sun, and the obstruction of such light by architectural elements. Screens are the most common examples of these elements which are used to diffuse light and create shadows. Susceptible to every nuanced change in the direction and intensity of light, these screens exhibit a great diversity of finishes and ornamentation. Eaves carvings, like

Shadows add to the richness of floor textures.

Left & right: Manipulation of light, shadow and pattern is an important aspect of Asian aesthetic tradition.

Opposite: Timber pergolas create a dense network of shadows.

The play of shadows on brickwork has been used to great effect here.

those found in Malay and Thai architecture, also illustrate the use of architectural details to shape a chiaroscuro that changes throughout the day with light. Burmese temples, with their gingerbread eaves, cast especially distinctive shadows.

Footnotes:

1 Jun'ichiro Tanizaki, *In Praise of Shadows*, translated by Thomas J. Harper and Edward G. Seidensticker, Charles E. Tuttle Company, Inc, Tokyo, 1990, pp. 18

Left & right: In traditional Thai architecture, the precision of craftsmanship is unmistakable under the intensity of natural light.

An elaborately carved
Balinese door, with its
rich texture highlighted
by falling light.

Corridors are animated by the shifting interplay of patterns.

Shadows cast onto walls and window openings.

Colored planes are susceptible to every nuanced change in the direction of light.

The Malaysian state Pahang's Kuantan-Cherating belt is one of the most popular locations for tourists to the east coast of Malaysia. Its long stretches of sandy beaches are lapped by clear waters of the South China Sea and dotted with many beach resorts.

The Impiana Resort, designed by Malaysian architect Jimmy Lim, is one of the latest luxurious properties that have sprouted up in the rapidly developing area. Derived from the Malay word *impian*, which means "dream", Impiana Resort is located about 45 km north of Kuantan on the road to Kemaman in Trengganu. The client's brief was to create an intimate resort that conjures up images of traditional Malay fishing villages on the east coast.

The architectural strategy attempts to cluster the richly convival public facilities and food outlets around a central pool area.

As the east coast is subjected to annual flooding during the monsoon season, these major spaces are raised four metres above the surrounding ground level. A total of 250 seaview deluxe rooms and suites are carefully designed to spread over 12 hectares of lush greenery. The surrounding vegetation is mainly hardy shrubs and mangrove swamps.

There are 142 deluxe rooms, seven suites and one sumptuous suite. Sixty three-bedroom chalets and 40 two-bedroom chalets are also designed to supplement the typical guestroom blocks. A variety of room layouts is achieved by staggering the different levels.

All the major roof elements and structures are inspired by traditional forms. The main reception area consists of a single-volume pitched space about 14 metres high. The roof is built of timber trusses braced and bracketed to create a voluminous structure. Skylights, as well as gaps between the fragmented layered roofs, allow diffused natural light into the space, creating a changing light-filled environment at various times of the day. The roof over the lounge at the reception lobby is lowered to provide a greater sense of intimacy, which at the same time produces a rich quality of texture, light and shade.

The resort is designed to take advantage of the long beach frontage. All rooms are oriented in an easterly direction for views. The buildings are also set back 60 metres from the high water mark. They are raised above the ground level to minimise earthworks as well as to allow free flow of surface water. Huge

Top: Spread over 12 hectares, the sprawling resort is inspired by the traditional architecture of Malaysia.

earthernware jars are placed at all entrances to guestrooms. This is to encourage guests to wash their feet before entering the room – a traditional practice in Malay villages.

In the pursuit of a return to the essentials of vernacular architecture based on an immediate sensual engagement with natural materials, the result at the Impiana is rather mixed. It clearly lacks the effusive lyricism found in Lim's smaller projects. The low-rise forms are much more successful than the medium-rise structures, demonstrating keenly the problematic issue of using pitched roofs in tall structures.

Building heights are staggered to achieve greater informality.

All rooms are oriented in an easterly direction for views.

Water features play an important role at the resort.

The reception lobby has a voluminous space roofed by an elaborate system of brackets and trusses.

Entrance pathway to the house consists of lava sandstone pavers.

Located in San Pe Sear, this exquisite residence has a heavy air of the passage of time. It has a subtle interplay of light and shade that is reminiscent of the highly evocative traditional Vietnamese house featured in the movie *Scent of the Green Papaya*. The owner, who is a royal princess, has an amazing collection of Thai artefacts which are carefully displayed throughout the house. But perhaps the most impressive aspect of this elegant house is the pervading presence of light and shadows.

Demonstrating a keen sensitivity to Lanna culture, the architect has given the client a delightful structure that is a refined evocation of dwelling. Liberal use of timber screens gives the house its magical quality of chiaroscuro and ever-changing moods. Filigree patterns of light frame the owner's honed collection of heirlooms and antiques. The miscellany of artworks and curios, set in niches or incorporated into the structure of the house, also adds immeasurably to the overall ambience.

The capacious rooms, panelled in aged and mellow teak, hark back to the unhurried refinement of another era. An overall languorous quality pervades the whole composition. The outcome is a handsomely detailed residence of great confidence and competence, where site, form and materials have been integrated into an indissoluble and beguiling whole.

A central courtyard forms the focus of the house.

The use of screens and wide eaves gives the house its magical quality of chiaroscuro and ever-changing moods.

A miscellany of artworks adds immeasurably to the house's ambience.

Next page: Timber screens frame the court-yard.

Conceptualised by the Perth-based team of Grounds Kent Architects, the architects responsible for the highly successful Four Seasons Bali at Jimbaran, this boutique hotel is located in the barren north coast of Bali.

It is situated to take advantage of one of Bali's best scuba and snorkelling locations. The wreck of an American Liberty ship is situated a few hundred metres along the beach from the hotel. This is a magnet for the marine life and supports a great diversity of fish and corals.

A gateway leads to a temple sited next to the resort.

Like a mysterious walled compound, the meandering assemblage of tightly clustered pavilions reveals itself slowly. Space folds and enfolds as one moves through the compound, revealing views and extending perceptions. Lushly landscaped gardens make the resort appear much bigger than it actually is. There is a dive school incorporated into the facilities. An intimate restaurant overlooks a small knife-edged swimming pool.

Traditional materials are employed throughout the entire compound.

Right: A small pool is located next to the beach.

*Textured walls provide
privacy for every villa.*

The 16 pavilions are intimate and inward-looking. Located next to the beach, the incessant pounding of waves creates a highly atmospheric environment. With much discipline, the architect has interwoven sensitivity and simplicity to create a thoughtful piece of work within a really cramped site. Unfortunately, it is perhaps too small a canvas for the architects to exhibit their full repertoire of skills that were employed with such subtle effects at the Four Seasons Jimbaran.

Intimate courtyards are a recurring theme.

View of the beach villa from the garden.

Located 45 km northeast of Kanyan Kumari, or commonly known as Cape Comorin, this beguiling timber palace is one of the most beautiful works of architecture in South India. Kanyan Kumari, situated in the state of Tamil Nadu, is the southern-most tip of India. This town is also fairly near the popular resort city of Trivandrum in the state of Kerala.

This part of the subcontinent has remained relatively untouched by the wave of foreign invasions through the centuries. It has thus evolved a distinctive culture that is characterised by a certain exuberance. Geographically, this stretch of India is also unique. Sandy beaches, lined with coconut groves, offer an idyll tropical setting.

The vast Padmanabhapuram Palace was the seat of the ancient rulers of Travancore who ruled from A.D. 849 to 1333. Individual buildings, linked by elaborate bridges and intermediate structures, are characterised by white walls, dark timber elements and steeply pitched roofs with wide overhangs. Like a cryptic maze, the entire complex consists of an elaborate sequence of individual rooms and narrow corridors punctuated by transitional semi-outdoor terraces. Workmanship is remarkably fine throughout. The Palace is also famous for its black floors which are made from an unusually strange concoction of ash and egg white. Exquisite murals and sculptures can also be found throughout the complex.

Richly carved details of a typical column.

Opposite top: The complex of buildings is characterised by the pervasive use of white walls and steeply pitched roofs.

Opposite bottom: Open-sided corridors linked the entire complex in an elaborate manner.

Architectural elements are juxtaposed in an intriguing manner.

These exquisite buildings, ranging in scale from the grandiose to the intimate, enclose tiny sunken courtyards filled with luminosity. Richly nuanced, the Palace's timber structures enclose and dissolve space with light and shadow. Throughout, there is a feeling of space being condensed and then expanded with irresistible charm. An intriguingly cacophonous ensemble, the Palace combines sensual and metaphoric worlds. It is a magnificent complex of great delicacy and subtlety.

The interiors are filled with luminosity from filtered light.

Elaborate and fine details are evident throughout the complex.

Finely carved brackets support horizontal timber screens.

SYNTHESIS

*"If architects are to continue to
do useful work on this planet,
then surely their proper concern must be the creation of
place – the ordered imposition
of man's self on specific locations across the face of the
earth. To make a place is to
make a domain that helps
people know where they are
and by extension who they
are."*

Charles Moore

Nusa Dua, Bali, Indonesia.

*Opposite: An architecture
that is firmly anchored
to both place and time
provides an ineluctable
physical experience.*

Architecture bears cultural meaning. Mies van der Rohe perhaps articulated it most succinctly when he urged that "present and past must be compared for differences and similarities in both a material and spiritual sense. This is why the buildings of the past must be studied and vividly described so as to convey a clear grasp of their essentials. It is not merely a matter of taking their greatness and significance as an architectural criterion

but also of realising that they were bound to a particular non-recurrent historical situation and thus place us under a duty to aspire to our own creative achievements."[1] But many architects have continued to dismiss the use of local culture as folkloric and marginal to theoretical discourse.

Any discussion on a place-specific architecture will inevitably lead to the obligatory theme of the now hackneyed term "regionalism". But the lesson remains that the architectural strategy for design in the tropics should not be to simply imitate vernacular forms. Precedents cannot be merely *transferred.*

Their underlying principles of form and construction need to be abstracted, generalised and *transformed* into meaningful works appropriate for contemporary use and context. Such works transcend aspects of style and possess a presence beyond the legibility of cultural codes.

Susannah Hagan argues that "regionalism requires first, an understanding of what went before in a particular place, whether vernacular or designed, and second, the sophiscation to be able to allude to it abstractly rather than to quote it literally. Too many architects are prevented by ideology and/or a lack of talent from fulfilling these conditions. But as models for students instinctively leaning towards such a strategy, the architects who do fulfil these conditions, the Correas and the Chadirjis, are more valuable to the world's multeity than any number of more 'up-to-date' figures on the scene."[2]

The concept of regionalism is not a static one. Like all other works of art, this concept is defined and re-defined by each new work that takes its inspiration from the past.

The use of local culture has been too readily dismissed as marginal to theoretical discourse.

Top: Dusit Santiburi, Ko Samui, Thailand.

Tanah Gajah, Bali, Indonesia.

The Regent Chiang Mai, Thailand.

Previous page: The Regent
Chiang Mai, Thailand.

Milan Kundera, in his engagingly poetic *Testaments Betrayed : An Essay in Nine Parts*, argues that "great works can only be born within the history of their art and as *participants* in that history. It is only inside history that we can see what is new and what is repetitive, what is discovery and what is imitation; in other words, only inside history can a work exist as a *value* capable of being discerned and judged. Nothing seems to me worse for art than to fall outside its own history, for it is a fall into the chaos where aesthetic values can no longer be perceived."[3]

The majority of architects have not yet realised the potential poetry inherent in using modern technologies to synthesise a response to place and culture. At the same time, a response to the physical and an expression of the cultural cannot be seen as two separate issues. They

A response to the physical and an expression of the cultural cannot be seen as two seperate issues.

are intertwined in an indissoluble manner. The formal and poetic possibilities are thus immense. One must confront these impulses in order to challenge orthodox architectural practices. A truly tropical architecture is one that resolves them in a poetic manner and re-engages our senses. Such exhortations have been heard so many times. But as T.S Eliot puts it :

> " You say I am repeating
> Something I have said before.
> I shall say it again.
> Shall I say it again ? "

Footnotes:

1   Werner Blaser, *Mies van der Rohe: the art of structure*, Birkhäuser Verlag, Basel,1993, pp. 53

2   Susannah Hagan, "Whatever happened to regionalism ?" in *The Architectural Review*, February 1994, pp. 73

3   Milan Kundera, *Testaments Betrayed: An Essay in Nine Parts*, Harper Collins Publishers, New York, 1995, pp.18

The Impiana Resort, Cherating, Malaysia.

Opened in 1973, the 390-room Bali Hyatt is located in Sanur, a former fishing village and home to Brahman priests. Built on a former coconut plantation of over 2000 trees, with a 500-metre long white beach, the hotel is probably one of the most important architectural precedents for all subsequent hotels in Bali.

Touted by the management for "its authenticity and its unique Balinese ambience", the hotel has always been considered a 'classic' property. The place has an ancient charm, redolent of scenes from a bygone era. It also demonstrates convincingly how the architecture of a large hotel can assume an unobtrusive role in the landscape.

Designed by the Hong Kong-based Palmer and Turner, the simple architecture is successfully integrated into 15 hectares of spectacular landscaped gardens. These gardens, sensitively designed oases full of surprises, add immeasurably to the ambience of the hotel. This concept of lush landscaping was further reinforced by the establishment of the Tropical Horticultural Garden of decorative plants in 1983 which houses the hotel's wide collection of tropical plants.

In 1981, a new phase of planting and design was carried out by landscape architect Michael White, his associate Ketut Marsa and a large team of gardeners. Stone carvings and other objects by Bali's renowned sculptors were added to complement the brilliant displays of tropical abundance.

The architecture of the hotel is fundamentally straightforward and manages to preserve in the interiors the languorous feeling of its beautiful landscaped gardens. Its low-key guestroom blocks are housed in three courts while the lobby pavilion is a voluminous structure inspired by the traditional Balinese meeting hall. Supported by timber columns, the huge thatched roof is a unique feature amongst large hotels.

The hotel was closed for renovation and a general facelift programme during the latter half of 1994. Hirsch Bedner and Associates was commissioned as interior designers for the rejuvenation of all existing guestrooms. The hotel's US$12 million restoration project retains much of the original character and atmosphere, yet augmenting and upgrading facilities to keep abreast of new developments in the hotel

A new Regency Club Lounge was built over a landscaped pool.

Opposite: The hotel is successfully integrated into 15 hectares of spectacular landscaped gardens.

industry. The interior designers were given a brief that says "at all costs, to preserve the classic Balinese character of the hotel".

The highlight of the renovation programme was the transformation of 50 superior rooms into the deluxe Regency Club class. Intricate batik and ikat fabrics are used in a rich palette of colours for upholstery and wall-hangings. A new Regency Club Lounge was also constructed over an artificial lake, amidst the existing gardens. Public spaces were also carefully restored. Wood finishes were taken back to their original finishes, where paint and varnishes were removed.

Despite being one of the early forerunners of hotels in Bali, the Bali Hyatt is still arguably one of the most well-designed hotels. Its splendid gardens demonstrate the possibilities and potential of architecture playing a secondary but critical supporting role to landscape design in the tropics.

All the public areas were restored to their original finishes.

Top & bottom: Rooms were renovated in a rich palette of colours.

The Republic of Maldives has been touted as the world's last remaining island paradise. Its natural attractions of sparkling white beaches and crystal-clear waters, teeming with an abundance of marine life, provide a magnet for tourists.

Club Med Maldives has undergone many facelifts since it first opened in 1973.

An archipelago in the Indian Ocean, the Maldives comprises 26 atolls and some 1,200 gem-like islands, of which only about 200 are inhabited. Under various types of leasehold agreements, 74 islands have been set aside exclusively for resort development, thus segregating tourists from the bulk of the indigenous Muslim population.

Each resort is located on a small uninhabited island to restrict the perceived negative impact of tourism on the host culture. Apart from the resorts and the capital city of Male, the rest of the islands are out of bounds to tourists. No form of transport exist between the islands, except the resorts' boats, which only transfer guests to and from the airport, itself on an island of its own. The sense of isolation is thus pervasive and can be positively delightful or frustratingly claustrophobic.

Maldives has been marketed as a tourist destination soley on the basis of its clear waters and marine life. The limited number of suitable islands for tourist development may, paradoxically, be the critical factor that can protect the long-term interests of the industry. There has been a growing problem with pollution, due largely to the indiscriminate dumping of cans. Fortunately, the destruction of the island's coral reefs and marine life has been contained with a fair amount of success. Perhaps the greatest threat – if predictions by scientists are accurate – is that of global warming. A slight rise in sea level in thirty years or so may be sufficient to submerge most of Maldives' low-lying islands which are less than two metres above sea level.

Located mainly within the North and South Male and Ari atolls, each resort is a self-contained island with its own facilities. Most of them are small, ranging in size from 10 to 50 rooms. Several big ones include Bandos Island Resort (221 rooms), Kuredhdhoo Island Resort (250 rooms) and Meeru Island Resort (214 rooms). Guest villas, which are either spread out along the perimeter of the island or built on stilts out at sea, usually consist of one or two rooms clustered under a common roof.

The architecture of many hastily constructed resorts attempts to project a romantic image of traditional Maldivian building styles. Walls built of white-washed coral are ubiquitous. Villas are often circular in shape with roofs made from *cadjan*, which are thatched palms bound by coir ropes. Many villas also have Balinese-style out-door baths. Like the problematic nature of resort architecture elsewhere, vernacular forms are removed from their social contexts and presented to tourists as icons of nostalgia and authenticity.

Club Med Farukolufushi departs in this respect. Instead of coral walls, it has timber pavilion structures that are ostensibly inspired by Sri Lankan architecture. They are especially reminiscent of the Sima Malaka Temple on Beira Lake in Colombo. These structures, housing the public facilities like dining rooms and bars, contrast sharply with the rough-hewn, double storey blocks of white-washed guest rooms.

First opened in 1973 with 112 rooms, the resort has undergone many facelifts. The most recent one occurred after the original main reception pavilion was burnt down. This intriguing structure, with its lithingly curved thatched roof, was replaced by new timber pavilions.

Designed with deference to the crystal-clear waters, the timber pavilions are probably the most intriguing part of the resort. The articulate use of timber brackets creates a shifting inter-play of light and shadows. Looking slightly out of place in the context, the building neverthe-less is beguiled by an explicit attention to detail and craftsmanship.

Timber brackets and bamboo blinds create an interesting play of shadows.

Each pavilion is disting-uished by immaculate craftsmanship.

After the original main reception pavilion was burnt down, the resort was renovated, including the swimming pool.

A sense of uninvaded
calm prevails throughout
the resort.

View of the bar and courtyard from one of the pavilions.

Guestroom blocks are designed without fuss.

Top: Poolside deck and bar pavilion.

Crystal-clear waters of
Maldives.

Mae Rim, one of the more scenic districts of Chiang Mai, boasts a number of tourist attractions like orchid gardens, rose gardens, butterfly farms and elephant centres. Misty hills, lush forests and winding streams provide a picturesque backdrop to the place. Many residence-cum-resort homes have been built to attract Thais from other parts of the country.

One of them is Baan Rimtai Saitarn, which means "House at the Downstream". It is designed by Bangkok-based architect, Nithi Sthapitanonda of Architects 49. Located on the Mae Rim-Samoeng Old Road, about 800 metres from its junction with the Chotana Highway, the project is sandwiched by the Mae Sa and Lum Muang streams. It covers approximately 89 *rai* (36 acres) of former rice fields. The expansive land, previously terraced to trap water, has an interesting undulating terrain.

The project consists of specially designed houses, each sited to take advantage of the views. Many of them are also designed around lotus ponds and flowing streams which provide an animated aural ambience. One of these houses – Baan Pa Sang – won the Gold Medal Award from the Association of Siamese Architects in 1994. The citation reads :" The house is inspired by the dream of having a vacation house in the ideal atmosphere of the North . . . The plan is designed after a traditional Lanna multi-units house . . . the landscape is totally in harmony with the architecture."

The entire development, with its manicured houses and fine gardens, has an open park-like atmosphere. A communal recreational hall, or *sala*, located in middle of a pond, acts as a landmark in the setting. Its unique multi-tiered roof is based on the traditional styles of the region.

Houses are sited to take advantage of the undulating terrain and wonderful views.

Top: The communal recreational hall is the focus of the complex.

Left & right: All the specially designed houses are inspired by the traditional architecture of Northern Thailand.

The entire development, with its manicured houses and new gardens, is quietly spectacular.

The open, park-like setting of the complex is marked by the multi-tiered structure of the communal hall.

Fenestration treatment of one of the houses.

Top: Timber decks linking different pavilions can be found in many of the houses.

Nine villas are spread out across an undulating site.

Right: Courtyard of one of the houses.

M. R. Pannapa Chumpoonuj, a member of the royal family, plays a major role in helping architect Chulathat Kitibutr conceive the concept for the development of this exquisite neighbourhood of palatial compounds. The collaboration has resulted in a unique setting. Located in the cool highlands of Chiang Mai, the complex was developed as a single entity. The approach route takes the visitor through a scenic winding road surrounded by thickly forested hills.

Designed as a hillside retreat, the project is site-specific. There are nine villas, mostly consisting of 3 bedrooms, spread out across a large expanse of undulating hills. The balanced ensemble is skilfully sited and efficiently planned. Temperature drops to about 13 deg C during the "winter" months from November to January. The fireplace thus forms a focus in the design of the individual units.

Landscape features also draw on varied European influences. Meticulously clipped shrubs and a melange of sculptural pieces dominate the gardens. Each house has a *sala* or communal gazebo to take maximum advantage of the picturesque views. Carefully constructed views also offer surprises at various vantage points throughout the estate.

Carefully constructed
views offer surprises at
various vantage points
throughout the estate.

Landscape pools meander across the languid setting.

One of the many figurines in the site.

Sculpted objects are placed throughout the sprawling grounds.

" What we may accept as reality

cannot possibly be what we see

ready-made around us, but much

more what we attempt to visualise

in a dream, all of us together and

each of us separately, the dream of

a new - truly new - life, shaped like

a poem. "

Aris Konstantinidis

BIBLIOGRAPHY

Gaston Bachelard, *The Poetics of Space*, Beacon Press, Boston, 1969.

Kenneth Frampton, *Studies in Tectonic Culture*, MIT Press, 1995.

Steven Holl, "The Matter(s) of Architecture" in *Hariri & Hariri,* The Monacelli Press, Inc., New York, 1995.

Kishio Kurokawa, "Rikyu Gray and the Art of Ambiguity" in *The Japan Architect*, June 1979.

Juhanni Pallasmaa, "Six Themes For The Next Millenium" in *The Architecture Review*, July 1994.

Juhani Pallasmaa, "An Architecture of the Seven Senses" in *Questions of Perception*, A+U Architecture and Urbanism, July 1994 Special Issue.

Robert Powell, *The Tropical Asian House*, Select Books Pte Ltd, Singapore, 1996.

Christian Norberg-Schulz, *Genius Loci: Towards a Phenomenology of Architecture*, Rizzoli Intgernational Publications, Inc., New York, 1980.

Tan Hock Beng, *Tropical Architecture and Interiors*, Page One Publishing Pte Ltd, Singapore, 1994.

Tan Hock Beng, *Tropical Resorts*, Page One Publishing Pte Ltd, Singapore, 1995.

Jun'ichiro Tanizaki, *In Praise of Shadows* , translated by Thomas J. Harper and Edward G. Seidensticker, Charles E. Tuttle Company, Inc, Tokyo, 1990.

PHOTO CREDITS

(All photographs are taken by Tan Hock Beng except those listed below)

P 8	Bensley Design Studios	P 98	Maria Hartati
P 11	Novotel Benoa,	P 100-103	Sangwan and Rittirong,
	Bensley Design Studios		Bensley Design Studios
P 12	K C Sin	P 105	Chan Soo Khian
P 16	Bensley Design Studios	P112-115	Albert Lim,
P 18	Maria Hartati		Richard Ho Architects
P 25	Bensley Design Studios	P 116-121	Ace Commercial
P 34	Bunnag Architects	P130-134	Chan Soo Khian
P 42	Bunnag Architects	P 138	Chan Soo Khian
P 46	Bunnag Architects	P142-147	Chan Soo Khian
P 53	Bensley Design Studios	P 163	Chan Soo Khian
P 58-63	Bunnag Architects	P 167	Maria Hartati
P 73	Maria Hartati	P 169	Anura Ratnavibhushana
P 75-77	Anura Ratnavibhushana	P 170-173	Luca Invernizzi Tettoni,
P 80	Bensley Design Studios		CSL Associates
P 86-89	Xiao Photo Workshop	P 187	Bunnag Architects

ACKNOWLEDGEMENTS

Completing this third book has not been any easier than the first two. It is just as arduous but equally rewarding task. Many people have shared their time and profound knowledge with me. Their experiences, insights and friendships have been a great inspiration. I also drew upon insights and theoretical frameworks from a wide range of disciplines and scholars in the social sciences and humanities, as well as the poetic musings on architecture by Juhani Pallasmaa and the academic rigour of Kenneth Frampton.

I would like to thank my publisher, Mark Tan, who once again initiated the early ideas, as well as Violet Tan for her ability to co-ordinate so many different things at the same time. K C Sin has also done a marvellous job in the layout of the book. For reading and responding to various parts of the book, and for their honest opinions, I owe tremendous debts to many friends who have contributed in unchartable ways. In particular, I wish to thank Sheila Oliveiro for copy-editing the manuscript. I am also indebted to two good friends, Bill Bensley and Lek Bunnag . Their exquisite works are a delight. They have also provided constant support and assistance throughout the project. Bensley's office, and in particular P. Kheuwadee, have contributed beautiful renderings for each of the chapter's entrance page.

I would also like to extend my appreciation to Robert Powell for his support during my years of learning, tutoring, writing and now practice. Another friend, M.L.Chainimit Navarat, has keenly provided assistance whenever it was needed. Many others are always ready with encouragement and help. They include William Lim, Karan Grover, Jimmy Lim, Lok Wooi, Kerry Hill, Ernesto Bedmar, Kevin Tan, Richard Ho, Chan Soo Khian, Guy Setiadi, Sunshine Wong, Hendra Hadiprana, Sindhu Hadiprana, Anura and Sundarika Ratnavibhushana.

I wish also to extend my particular gratitude to many others who have helped in making my trips and photography sessions so much more easier and enjoyable. Among these, particular credit should be accorded to Foo May Leng, Nareerat Srisawat, Chulathat Kitibutr, Nithi Sthapitanonda, M.R. Pannapa Chumpoonuj, Napaporn Sranpat, Karl Princic, Agus Wawo-Runtu, Cecilia Leong-Faulkner, Marc Hediger, Willie Ooi, Intan Petersen, Martin Grounds, Glenn Parker, Vera Warouw, Narima Yusof, Wirya Santoso, Steve Scott, Stephen Lomax, Peter Khong, Kora Amalwati, Joseph Zitnik, Florian Hallermann, Charlotte Yasa, I Wayan Rija, Simon Hirst, Lee Sutton, Liza Chang, Christophe Lajus and Mark Kissner.

Most of all, my gratitude goes to my family : Maria, Brent and Gale. They have been the powerful leading forces behind its completion.

Tan Hock Beng
Singapore, October 1996